# Shakespeare

# King Henry IV

## Part 2

Edited by Rex Gibson

Series Editor: Rex Gibson
Director, Shakespeare

DISCARD

CAMBRIDGE
UNIVERSITY PRESS

PUBLISHED BY THE PRESS SYNDICATE OF THE UNIVERSITY OF CAMBRIDGE
The Pitt Building, Trumpington Street, Cambridge CB2 1RP, United Kingdom

CAMBRIDGE UNIVERSITY PRESS
The Edinburgh Building, Cambridge CB2 2RU, United Kingdom
40 West 20th Street, New York, NY 10011–4211, USA
10 Stamford Road, Oakleigh, Melbourne 3166, Australia

First published 1999

Printed in the United Kingdom at the University Press, Cambridge

Typeset in Ehrhardt

*A catalogue record for this book is available from the British Library*

*Library of Congress Cataloguing in Publication data applied for*

ISBN 0 521 62688 9

Prepared for publication by Stenton Associates
Designed by Richard Morris, Stonesfield Design
Picture research by Callie Kendall

# Contents

# Cambridge School Shakespeare

This edition of *Henry IV Part 2* is part of the *Cambridge School Shakespeare* series. Like every other play in the series, it has been specially prepared to help all students in schools and colleges.

This *Henry IV Part 2* aims to be different from other editions of the play. It invites you to bring the play to life in your classroom, hall or drama studio through enjoyable activities that will increase your understanding. Actors have created their different interpretations of the play over the centuries. Similarly, you are encouraged to make up your own mind about *Henry IV Part 2*, rather than having someone else's interpretation handed down to you.

*Cambridge School Shakespeare* does not offer you a cut-down or simplified version of the play. This is Shakespeare's language, filled with imaginative possibilities. You will find on every left-hand page: a summary of the action, an explanation of unfamiliar words, and a choice of activities on Shakespeare's language, characters and stories.

Between each act and in the pages at the end of the play, you will find notes, illustrations and activities. These will help to increase your understanding of the whole play.

There are a large number of activities to give you the widest choice to suit your own particular needs. Please don't think you have to do every one. Choose the activities that help you most.

This edition will be of value to you whether you are studying for an examination, reading for pleasure, or thinking of putting on the play to entertain others. You can work on the activities on your own or in groups. Many of the activities suggest a particular group size, but don't be afraid to make up smaller or larger groups to suit your own purposes.

Although you are invited to treat *Henry IV Part 2* as a play, you don't need special dramatic or theatrical skills to do the activities. By choosing your activities, and by exploring and experimenting, you can make your own interpretations of Shakespeare's language, characters and stories. Whatever you do, remember that Shakespeare wrote his plays to be acted, watched and enjoyed.

Rex Gibson

This edition of *Henry IV Part 2* uses the text of the play established by Giorgio Melchiori in *The New Cambridge Shakespeare*.

# Before the play begins

*Henry IV Part 2* continues the story, begun in *Part 1*, of the rebellions against King Henry. His troubled reign began when, as Bullingbrook, he seized the throne of England from Richard II, and probably ordered Richard's murder. The play enacts Shakespeare's version of the power struggles in early fifteenth-century England caused by Henry's dubious claim to be the rightful king.

*Part 2* begins shortly after the battle of Shrewsbury in 1403. It imaginatively dramatises certain events between that time and 1413, when King Henry IV died and his son, Prince Hal, succeeded him as King Henry V.

*Part 1* had left unfinished business. Henry had defeated one rebellion led by Hotspur, but the play ended with him preparing to meet another rebel army led by the Archbishop of York. Prince Hal had vowed to throw off his wild ways and to break from his corrupt companion Falstaff. *Part 2* sees the defeat of the Archbishop's rebellion and the working out of Hal's vow. It ends with Hal crowned as King Henry V and his final rejection of Falstaff.

Shakespeare did far more in *Parts 1* and *2* than portray the military and political events of the unquiet times of Henry IV. His dramatic imagination created the character who would ensure the plays' lasting success from the moment of their first performance: Falstaff.

## The cycle of Shakespeare's history plays (1398–1485)

*Richard II*: Bullingbrook deposes King Richard and is crowned as King Henry IV. Hal is briefly mentioned.

*Henry IV Parts 1* and *2*: Rebellions against Henry are defeated. Hal enjoys Falstaff's company, but, crowned as King Henry V, rejects him.

*Henry V*: Henry is victorious at Agincourt and is betrothed to Katherine, the French King's daughter.

*Henry VI Parts 1, 2* and *3*: Henry VI loses the English possessions in France. His kingdom is racked by the Wars of the Roses. Henry is murdered by Richard, Duke of Gloucester.

*Richard III*: Richard murders his way to the English throne, but is overthrown by Richmond who becomes Henry VII.

# The world of the play

# List of characters

RUMOUR  the presenter

## The Court

KING HENRY IV
PRINCE HAL
PRINCE JOHN OF LANCASTER
DUKE OF GLOUCESTER
DUKE OF CLARENCE
} King Henry's sons

LORD CHIEF JUSTICE

EARL OF WARWICK
EARL OF WESTMORELAND
EARL OF SURREY
GOWER
HARCOURT
SIR JOHN BLUNT

## The Rebels

ARCHBISHOP OF YORK
EARL OF NORTHUMBERLAND
LADY NORTHUMBERLAND
LADY PERCY
  Northumberland's daughter-in-law
COLEVILE OF THE DALE

LORD MOWBRAY
LORD HASTINGS
LORD BARDOLPH

TRAVERS
MORTON

## The Tavern

SIR JOHN FALSTAFF
BARDOLPH
PISTOL
} Followers of Falstaff
POINS Prince Hal's friend
PETO Prince Hal's follower
PAGE to Falstaff

HOSTESS QUICKLY
DOLL TEARSHEET
FRANCIS
WILL
} Drawers (Barmen)
FANG
SNARE
} Officers

## Gloucestershire

SHALLOW
SILENCE
} Justices (Magistrates)
DAVY  Shallow's servant

MOULDY
SHADOW
WART
FEEBLE
BULLCALF
} Falstaff's recruits

Grooms, Servants, Porter, Messenger, Officers, musicians, soldiers

The action of the play takes place at various locations in England.

*Rumour tells how he spreads lies round all the world, sometimes of peace, sometimes of threatening war. Such false reports are easily spread, because everyone joins in rumour-mongering.*

## 1 Induction (in small groups)

An induction is a prologue, or explanation of what the play will be about. Rumour is a symbolic or allegorical figure of the kind often appearing in plays, pageants and masques from medieval times until after Shakespeare's death.

Rumour first gives a general account of what he does (lines 1–22), then talks directly about the play. Use the suggestions below and on page 6 to help you prepare a presentation of Rumour's lines.

a Design Rumour's costume, 'painted full of tongues' (see page 38).

b Rumours create a sense of unease and confusion. Experiment to find an appropriate tone of voice for Rumour (for example, contemptuously scornful and unpleasant, revelling in the ease with which he can make people believe and spread rumours).

c Work out gestures that Rumour might use to accompany his words. For example, at line 22, what action could he use to show that all the audience ('my household') are rumour-mongers?

## 2 Imagery: music and monsters

Lines 15–20 contain two vivid images. Rumour is pictured as a musical instrument like a recorder. It is played upon by rumours ('Blown by surmises'), spreading lies inspired by jealousy. The pipe is so easy to play ('so plain a stop') that any mob or crowd ('blunt monster with uncounted heads') can use it.

Make up several lines of your own, beginning 'Rumour is ...', which suggest similarly telling pictures of how quickly rumours spread.

vent  holes
**Orient**  East
**post-horse**  hired horse
still  always
covert  hidden
**fearful musters**  panic-stricken recruitment of armies

**prepared defence**  preparations against invasion
big  pregnant
**And no such matter**  such rumours are false
anatomise  explain, dissect

# King Henry IV Part 2

*Enter* RUMOUR *painted full of tongues*

RUMOUR  Open your ears; for which of you will stop
      The vent of hearing when loud Rumour speaks?
      I from the Orient to the drooping West
      (Making the wind my post-horse) still unfold
      The acts commencèd on this ball of earth;        5
      Upon my tongues continual slanders ride,
      The which in every language I pronounce,
      Stuffing the ears of men with false reports:
      I speak of peace while covert enmity,
      Under the smile of safety, wounds the world;      10
      And who but Rumour, who but only I,
      Make fearful musters, and prepared defence,
      Whiles the big year, swoll'n with some other grief,
      Is thought with child by the stern tyrant War?
      And no such matter. Rumour is a pipe      15
      Blown by surmises, Jealousy's conjectures,
      And of so easy and so plain a stop
      That the blunt monster with uncounted heads,
      The still discordant wav'ring multitude,
      Can play upon it. But what need I thus      20
      My well-known body to anatomise
      Among my household? Why is Rumour here?

*Rumour tells the truth about what happened at the battle of Shrewsbury,
then describes the false rumours he has spread. In Scene 1, Lord
Bardolph arrives at the Earl of Northumberland's castle.*

## 1 Telling the truth (in small groups)

Rumour first says what actually happened at the battle of Shrewsbury:
King Henry (Harry) defeated the rebels led by Hotspur. In *Henry IV
Part 1*, Shakespeare's portrayal of the battle shows Prince Hal ('Harry
Monmouth') killing Hotspur and rescuing his father from death at the
hands of the Scottish warrior Douglas.

Rumour recounts how he has spread false reports everywhere,
claiming that King Henry and Prince Hal have been killed in the battle.
Rumour knows that to Northumberland, father of Hotspur, the lies
about the battle will be comforting but eventually hurtful ('smooth
comforts false').

a  Show the events described in lines 23–32 as two mimes to
   accompany Rumour's words. Your first mime shows what really
   happened (23–7), the second shows the false events as Rumour
   describes them.

b  Use Rumour's description of Warkworth Castle as 'this
   worm-eaten hold of raggèd stone' to design the set for Scene 1.

## 2 Playing the Porter

This is the Porter's only appearance in the play. If you played the part,
would you try to make the Porter into a truly memorable character for
the audience (for example, playing him very drunk, or outstandingly
insolent and surly)? Or do you think he should be played merely as a
someone whose only function is to introduce Lord Bardolph? Give
reasons for your decision.

---

field  battlefield
office  duty
noise abroad  spread rumours
  everywhere
anointed  sacred
peasant  rural

worm-eaten hold  decaying castle
crafty-sick  pretending to be ill
posts  messengers on horses
tiring on  worn out by furious
  riding

I run before King Harry's victory,
Who in a bloody field by Shrewsbury
Hath beaten down young Hotspur and his troops,                    25
Quenching the flame of bold rebellion
Even with the rebels' blood. But what mean I
To speak so true at first? My office is
To noise abroad that Harry Monmouth fell
Under the wrath of noble Hotspur's sword,                         30
And that the king before the Douglas' rage
Stooped his anointed head as low as death.
This have I rumoured through the peasant towns
Between that royal field of Shrewsbury
And this worm-eaten hold of raggèd stone,                         35
Where Hotspur's father, old Northumberland,
Lies crafty-sick. The posts come tiring on,
And not a man of them brings other news
Than they have learnt of me. From Rumour's tongues
They bring smooth comforts false, worse than true wrongs.         40

*Exit*

# ACT 1    SCENE 1
## Outside Warkworth Castle

*Enter the* LORD BARDOLPH *and the* PORTER

LORD BARDOLPH  Who keeps the gate here, ho? Where is the earl?
PORTER  What shall I say you are?
LORD BARDOLPH                    Tell thou the earl
That the Lord Bardolph doth attend him here.
PORTER  His worship is walked forth into the orchard,
Please it your honour knock but at the gate,                       5
And he himself will answer.

*Enter the Earl [of] NORTHUMBERLAND*

LORD BARDOLPH                    Here comes the earl.

*[Exit Porter]*

*Lord Bardolph is confident that the rebels won the battle of Shrewsbury. King Henry is near to death, Hal slain, Falstaff a prisoner, and all the rest fled. Travers brings different news.*

## 1 'What news?' (in groups of four)

Every history play has a special problem: how to ensure, right at the start, that the audience has sufficient information to make sense of what follows. Shakespeare chooses a particularly effective method of providing that information, showing that Rumour has done his work well.

Instead of having someone narrating past events, Shakespeare begins with Lord Bardolph's false story of the rebels' victory. He then has Travers provide a hearsay account. Finally, Morton provides an eyewitness account of the defeat of the rebels.

Take parts as Northumberland, Lord Bardolph, Travers and Morton and speak lines 7–135, in which the truth gradually emerges from contradictory accounts. Use the activities below and on pages 10–14 to help your understanding.

## 2 Echoes of Caesar

Suggest how line 21 echoes Julius Caesar's famous claim, 'I came, I saw, I conquered'.

## 3 Creating atmosphere (in small groups)

When you have read lines 7–135, talk together about the dramatic effectiveness of Shakespeare's method, particularly in the tense, uncertain atmosphere it creates. It will help if you begin by reminding yourselves that today television and radio report battles as they happen. Then identify the ways in which Shakespeare builds up an impression of a medieval world where eye-witness accounts are slow to arrive.

---

**stratagem** violent act
**contention** war
**the Blunts, Stafford** supporters of King Henry
**brawn, the hulk Sir John** fat boar, Falstaff
**good name** a noble family

**over-rode** overtook
**haply may retail** perhaps may tell
**Sir John Umfrevile** a rebel who does not appear in the play
**forspent** exhausted
**breathe** rest

NORTHUMBERLAND  What news, Lord Bardolph? Every minute now
        Should be the father of some stratagem;
        The times are wild: contention, like a horse
        Full of high feeding, madly hath broke loose,       10
        And bears down all before him.
LORD BARDOLPH               Noble earl,
        I bring you certain news from Shrewsbury.
NORTHUMBERLAND Good, and God will.
LORD BARDOLPH            As good as heart can wish:
        The king is almost wounded to the death,
        And, in the fortune of my lord your son,       15
        Prince Harry slain outright, and both the Blunts
        Killed by the hand of Douglas. Young Prince John
        And Westmoreland and Stafford fled the field,
        And Harry Monmouth's brawn, the hulk Sir John,
        Is prisoner to your son. O, such a day,       20
        So fought, so followed, and so fairly won,
        Came not till now to dignify the times
        Since Caesar's fortunes.
NORTHUMBERLAND          How is this derived?
        Saw you the field? Came you from Shrewsbury?
LORD BARDOLPH I spake with one, my lord, that came from thence,   25

               *Enter* TRAVERS

        A gentleman well bred, and of good name,
        That freely rendered me these news for true.
NORTHUMBERLAND Here comes my servant Travers, who I sent
        On Tuesday last to listen after news.
LORD BARDOLPH My lord, I over-rode him on the way,       30
        And he is furnished with no certainties
        More than he haply may retail from me.
NORTHUMBERLAND Now Travers, what good tidings comes with you?
TRAVERS My lord, Sir John Umfrevile turned me back
        With joyful tidings, and, being better horsed,     35
        Out-rode me. After him came spurring hard
        A gentleman, almost forspent with speed,
        That stopped by me to breathe his bloodied horse.
        He asked the way to Chester, and of him
        I did demand what news from Shrewsbury:       40

*Travers reports that he was told that Hotspur is dead. Bardolph denies the report is true. Morton arrives and Northumberland sees bad news written in his face.*

## 1 How does Travers tell his story?

Travers is a servant who has to report that he has heard news that his master's son (Harry Percy) is dead. Suggest what thoughts went through Traver's head as he rode back to Warkworth castle with his ominous news (for example, how to avoid using the word 'dead'?), and how he now feels in the presence of two mighty noblemen. Then explore different ways of speaking his lines 34–48.

## 2 Are appearances deceptive? (in pairs)

In *Macbeth*, King Duncan says 'there's no art to find the mind's construction in the face'. But Northumberland's three images in lines 60–73 show that he is confident that he can tell what Morton is thinking from the look on Morton's face:

'title-leaf' (line 60) – like the title page of a book or play that summarises the tragedy

'the strond' (line 62) – like the seashore which shows evidence of the retreating stormy tide

'Priam' (line 72) – like King Priam's face, when he woke to find Troy burning (in Greek mythology)

Talk together about whether you think that someone bringing bad news shows it in their face.

## 3 Should they laugh?

Morton brings an eye-witness account of the battle of Shrewsbury. If you were playing Morton, would you want the audience to laugh at your first four words?

---

**spur was cold** is dead
**jade** worn-out horse
**rowel head** spiked wheel on spur
**point** lace (used to fasten breeches)
**barony** noble title
**hilding** good-for-nothing, contemptible

**at a venture** recklessly
**a witnessed usurpation** evidence of the tide's attack
**party** forces, supporters
**apter** more significant

He told me that rebellion had bad luck,
And that young Harry Percy's spur was cold.
With that he gave his able horse the head,
And bending forwards struck his armèd heels
Against the panting sides of his poor jade                45
Up to the rowel head, and starting so
He seemed in running to devour the way,
Staying no longer question.
NORTHUMBERLAND                Ha? Again:
Said he young Harry Percy's spur was cold?
Of Hotspur, Coldspur? That rebellion                     50
Had met ill luck?
LORD BARDOLPH        My lord, I'll tell you what:
If my young lord your son have not the day,
Upon mine honour, for a silken point
I'll give my barony, never talk of it.
NORTHUMBERLAND Why should that gentleman that rode by Travers   55
Give then such instances of loss?
LORD BARDOLPH                      Who he?
He was some hilding fellow that had stol'n
The horse he rode on, and, upon my life,
Spoke at a venture. Look, here comes more news.

*Enter* MORTON

NORTHUMBERLAND Yea, this man's brow, like to a title-leaf,      60
Foretells the nature of a tragic volume:
So looks the strond whereon the imperious flood
Hath left a witnessed usurpation.
Say, Morton, didst thou come from Shrewsbury?
MORTON I ran from Shrewsbury, my noble lord,                    65
Where hateful death put on his ugliest mask
To fight our party.
NORTHUMBERLAND        How doth my son, and brother?
Thou tremblèst, and the whiteness in thy cheek
Is apter than thy tongue to tell thy errand.
Even such a man, so faint, so spiritless,                       70
So dull, so dead in look, so woe-begone,
Drew Priam's curtain in the dead of night,
And would have told him half his Troy had burnt:

*Northumberland fears that Morton's account of the battle will end in reports of death. He hopes his fears will prove unfounded, but expects the worst. Morton confirms that he saw Hotspur killed.*

## 1 The death of Hotspur (in pairs)

Morton has seen with his own eyes the death of Hotspur and the total defeat of the rebel army. He finally manages to give his report in lines 105–35. Write detailed notes for the actor advising him how to deliver his story (see also Activity 1 on page 14). Then step into role in turn as Morton and speak the lines.

## 2 Lord Bardolph's motives

Think of two or three reasons why Lord Bardolph was so keen to dismiss Travers' story (lines 51–4 and 56–9), and now disbelieves Morton's claim that Hotspur is dead.

## 3 Bringers of bad news (in pairs)

Talk together about the imagery that Northumberland uses in lines 100–3 ('losing office' could mean 'sorrowful duty' or 'dangerous role', and 'tolling' means 'ringing sadly for'). Tell each other whether you think the imagery accurately describes a messenger who brings bad news.

## 4 What's in a name?

Shakespeare sometimes gives his characters names which describe their personality or dramatic function (see page 201). Do you think he might have such thoughts in mind when he gave names to the two messengers who bring the fateful news? The French for death is 'mort', and 'traverse' means 'to cross'.

---

**my Percy** Hotspur
**brother** Worcester
**chanced** happened
**divination lies** guess is wrong
**gainsaid** lied to, contradicted

**belie** tell lies about
**faint quittance** weak repayment, feeble resistance
**never-daunted** always courageous

But Priam found the fire ere he his tongue,
And I my Percy's death ere thou report'st it.                    75
This thou wouldst say: 'Your son did thus and thus;
Your brother thus; so fought the noble Douglas –'
Stopping my greedy ear with their bold deeds.
But in the end, to stop my ear indeed,
Thou hast a sigh to blow away this praise,                        80
Ending with 'brother, son, and all are dead'.
MORTON Douglas is living, and your brother, yet;
But for my lord your son –
NORTHUMBERLAND                    Why, he is dead?
See, what a ready tongue suspicion hath:
He that but fears the thing he would not know        85
Hath by instinct knowledge from other's eyes
That what he feared is chanced. Yet speak, Morton,
Tell thou an earl his divination lies,
And I will take it for a sweet disgrace,
And make thee rich for doing me such wrong.          90
MORTON You are too great to be by me gainsaid,
Your spirit is too true, your fears too certain.
NORTHUMBERLAND  Yet for all this, say not that Percy's dead.
I see a strange confession in thine eye:
Thou shak'st thy head, and hold'st it fear, or sin        95
To speak a truth. If he be slain,
The tongue offends not that reports his death,
And he doth sin that doth belie the dead,
Not he which says the dead is not alive.
Yet the first bringer of unwelcome news                      100
Hath but a losing office, and his tongue
Sounds ever after as a sullen bell
Remembered, tolling a departing friend.
LORD BARDOLPH  I cannot think, my lord, your son is dead.
MORTON  I am sorry I should force you to believe          105
That which I would to God I had not seen,
But these mine eyes saw him in bloody state,
Rendering faint quittance, wearied and out-breathed,
To Harry Monmouth, whose swift wrath beat down
The never-daunted Percy to the earth,                         110
From whence with life he never more sprung up.

*Hotspur's death dispirited the rebel army which fled the battlefield. The king's army now threatens Northumberland. Hearing this, Northumberland throws off his illness and prepares to fight.*

## 1 Images of fire and flight (in pairs)

Morton briefly ('In few') tells how news of Hotspur's death, from the very first rumours ('Being bruited once') took away the rebel soldiers' will to fight. Lines 112–25 contain a complex cluster of contrasting images deriving from tempering (hardening) swords in fire, and the flight of bullets and arrows.

Work through the lines identifying how the imagery helps create the atmosphere of growing fear among the rebel army.

## 2 Battle reports

a In modern warfare, an officer writes a brief factual account of what happens each day in battle. Step into role as a rebel officer and write your account of what happened at the battle of Shrewsbury. Base your account on Morton's lines, in which Douglas, a Scottish warlord, is reported as slaying three knights disguised as King Henry ('th'appearance of the king'), but began to lose his courage ('Gan vail his stomach'), fled, and was captured.

b Ordinary soldiers usually have quite different recollections of a battle from that which appears in an official report. Write a letter home as a rebel soldier who fought at Shrewsbury.

## 3 Stage directions

Northumberland finds a kind of medicine ('physic') in the bad news. They spur him to throw off his illness and prepare for war. Find the stage directions that Shakespeare builds into Northumberland's lines, and use them to design a costume for him ('nice crutch' means unmanly support, a 'coif' is a nightcap or head bandage).

---

**fire and heat** bravery and motivation
**best-tempered** finest
**party** fellow rebels
**steeled** forged, given backbone
**abated** diminished

**enforcement** compulsion, given momentum
**keepers'** nurses'
**scaly gauntlet** armoured glove
**wanton** effeminate
**fleshed** inflamed

In few: his death, whose spirit lent a fire
Even to the dullest peasant in his camp,
Being bruited once, took fire and heat away
From the best-tempered courage in his troops,          115
For from his metal was his party steeled,
Which once in him abated, all the rest
Turned on themselves, like dull and heavy lead.
And as the thing that's heavy in itself
Upon enforcement flies with greatest speed,          120
So did our men, heavy in Hotspur's loss,
Lend to this weight such lightness with their fear
That arrows fled not swifter toward their aim
Than did our soldiers, aiming at their safety,
Fly from the field. Then was that noble Worcester          125
So soon ta'en prisoner, and that furious Scot,
The bloody Douglas, whose well-labouring sword
Had three times slain th'appearance of the king,
Gan vail his stomach, and did grace the shame
Of those that turned their backs, and in his flight          130
Stumbling in fear, was took. The sum of all
Is that the king hath won, and hath sent out
A speedy power to encounter you, my lord,
Under the conduct of young Lancaster
And Westmoreland. This is the news at full.          135

NORTHUMBERLAND  For this I shall have time enough to mourn.
In poison there is physic, and these news,
Having been well, that would have made me sick,
Being sick, have (in some measure) made me well.
And as the wretch whose fever-weakened joints,          140
Like strengthless hinges, buckle under life,
Impatient of his fit, breaks like a fire
Out of his keepers' arms, even so my limbs,
Weakened with grief, being now enraged with grief,
Are thrice themselves. Hence therefore thou nice crutch!          145
A scaly gauntlet now with joints of steel
Must glove this hand. And hence thou sickly coif,
Thou art a guard too wanton for the head
Which princes fleshed with conquest aim to hit.

> *Northumberland determines to let loose destruction on the world. His allies fear for his health, and Morton reminds him that he foresaw the risk of Hotspur's death. Lord Bardolph urges another rebellion.*

## 1 'Let Order die' (in pairs)

Lines 150–60 are an impassioned call for disorder to reign in England ('bloody courses' = violent action). An actor who played Northumberland said:

'He's really ranting here, full of fury at his son's death and determined to wreak havoc in England. When you speak it, you have to stress all the imperatives: "Now" and "Let" (which he uses five times). You start off slowly and emphatically, and build up to a madman's shout at the end.'

Use the actor's advice to deliver your own versions of the speech.

## 2 Echoes: theatre, the Bible, risk-taking

*Theatre and the Bible*: 'Time' and 'Spite' are personifications (see page 199). They often appeared as characters in medieval morality plays. Shakespeare also uses 'stage', 'act' and 'scene' in Northumberland's appeal for everyone to become like Cain, who, according to the Bible, killed his younger brother Abel.

*Risk-taking*: Morton uses 'you' or 'your' seven times as he strongly reminds Northumberland that he was fully aware of the risks involved before the rebellion began ('cast th'event'= calculated the risks). In lines 170–1 ('walked o'er perils'), Morton uses the same image of danger as that in *Henry IV Part 1* (Act 1 Scene 3, lines 188–92).

Lord Bardolph's lines 180–6 recall the Elizabethan merchant adventurers who hoped to make a ten-fold profit out of trading voyages. All the rebels knew the risks they were taking: the odds were 10:1 against success.

Look out for other echoes of Shakespeare's world as you read on.

---

**contention in a lingering act** long-drawn-out war
**complices** accomplices, comrades
**make head** raise an army
**presurmise** expectation
**dole of blows** battle, dealing out of blows

**capable/Of** liable to
**forward spirit** eager courage
**stiff-borne action** discipline of war
**wrought out life** succeeded
**o'er-set** defeated, gambling heavily
**body and goods** everything we have

Now bind my brows with iron, and approach          150
The ragged'st hour that Time and Spite dare bring
To frown upon th'enragèd Northumberland!
Let heaven kiss earth! Now let not Nature's hand
Keep the wild flood confined, let Order die,
And let this world no longer be a stage          155
To feed contention in a lingering act;
But let one spirit of the first-born Cain
Reign in all bosoms, that each heart being set
On bloody courses, the rude scene may end,
And darkness be the burier of the dead.          160
MORTON  This strainèd passion doth you wrong, my lord.
LORD BARDOLPH  Sweet earl, divorce not wisdom from your honour,
      The lives of all your loving complices
      Lean on your health, the which, if you give o'er
      To stormy passion, must perforce decay.          165
MORTON  You cast th'event of war, my noble lord,
      And summed the account of chance before you said
      'Let us make head.' It was your presurmise
      That in the dole of blows your son might drop.
      You knew he walked o'er perils, on an edge,          170
      More likely to fall in than to get o'er;
      You were advised his flesh was capable
      Of wounds and scars, and that his forward spirit
      Would lift him where most trade of danger ranged,
      Yet did you say 'Go forth'; and none of this,          175
      Though strongly apprehended, could restrain
      The stiff-borne action. What hath then befallen,
      Or what hath this bold enterprise brought forth,
      More than that being which was like to be?
LORD BARDOLPH  We all that are engagèd to this loss          180
      Knew that we ventured on such dangerous seas
      That if we wrought out life, 'twas ten to one;
      And yet we ventured, for the gain proposed
      Choked the respect of likely peril feared,
      And since we are o'er-set, venture again.          185
      Come, we will all put forth, body and goods.

*Morton reports that the Archbishop of York has raised another rebel army, and has assured its soldiers that God is on their side. Religious certainty now motivates a large army of all social classes.*

## 1 How to motivate a rebel army (in pairs)

Morton tells that the Archbishop's soldiers are far better motivated than Hotspur's defeated troops at Shrewsbury. Hotspur's soldiers did not fight wholeheartedly because they were rebels, and rebellion against a king could not be justified by religion (see page 191). Hotspur's soldiers believed that it was a sin to rebel, and would lead to their being damned in Hell for eternity.

In contrast, the Archbishop has inspired his rebel army with religious zeal ('Turns insurrection to religion'), and his soldiers now fight with body and soul ('a double surety'). The Archbishop proclaims that Henry IV committed a great sin in killing King Richard II at Pomfret (Pontefract) castle, so Heaven itself is against Henry, and anyone who fights against him has religion on his side.

**a** Speak Morton's lines as convincingly as you can.

**b** Today, many groups who fight against those who control their country call themselves 'freedom fighters', rather than 'rebels'. Identify some contemporary examples and discuss how you regard them: as rebels or as freedom fighters (see also page 108).

## 2 Shakespeare and history

Shakespeare compresses history to achieve dramatic effect. Scene 1 is set only a few days after the battle of Shrewsbury in 1403. But the Archbishop's rebellion did not take place until 1405. To discover other ways in which Shakespeare writes his own version of history, turn to page 202.

---

**well appointed powers** a strongly equipped army
**corpse** body
**potions** medicine
**insurrection** rebellion
**enlarge his rising** recruit other rebels
**Derives** justifies
**Bullingbrook** King Henry IV
**more and less** high- and low-status people
**posts** messengers on horses

MORTON  'Tis more than time; and, my most noble lord,
        I hear for certain and dare speak the truth:
        The gentle Archbishop of York is up
        With well appointed powers; he is a man                    190
        Who with a double surety binds his followers.
        My lord your son had only but the corpse,
        But shadows and the shows of men, to fight.
        For that same word, Rebellion, did divide
        The action of their bodies from their souls,               195
        And they did fight with queasiness, constrained
        As men drink potions, that their weapons only
        Seemed on our side; but for their spirits and souls,
        This word 'Rebellion' it had froze them up
        As fish are in a pond. But now the bishop                  200
        Turns insurrection to religion,
        Supposed sincere and holy in his thoughts;
        He's followed both with body and with mind,
        And doth enlarge his rising with the blood
        Of fair King Richard scraped from Pomfret stones:          205
        Derives from Heaven his quarrel and his cause,
        Tells them he doth bestride a bleeding land
        Gasping for life under great Bullingbrook,
        And more and less do flock to follow him.
NORTHUMBERLAND  I knew of this before, but, to speak truth,        210
        This present grief had wiped it from my mind.
        Go in with me, and counsel every man
        The aptest way for safety and revenge:
        Get posts and letters, and make friends with speed;
        Never so few, and never yet more need.                     215

                                                *Exeunt*

*Falstaff's tiny Page reports the doctor's ambiguous diagnosis.*
*Falstaff reflects that he causes other men to be witty. He jokes about his*
*Page and Prince Hal. His tailor refuses to grant him credit.*

## 1 Enter Sir John ... (in pairs)

Work out your own version of the entry stage direction to bring out the comic contrast of Falstaff and his Page. Falstaff is huge, the Page is tiny. In some productions the Page follows Falstaff, imitating his movements (he carries a 'buckler', a small round shield).

## 2 Falstaff's language (in pairs)

Speak lines 4–23 aloud several times to gain a first experience of Falstaff's style. You will find help with his language below and on each following left-hand page. Remember that being over-analytical can kill the humour, so don't keep pausing to work out every joke.

Falstaff begins by calling his tiny Page 'giant'. Such imaginative comic contrasts are one of the typical characteristics of his humour. Another of Falstaff's favourite methods is to pick on a person and make jokes and puns about him. Here, he starts with 'men of all sorts', then moves on to his Page, then to Prince Hal.

lines 4–7 Try a mock-sorrowful tone, or puzzled, or logical.

lines 7–14 Falstaff jokes on the size of his tiny Page ('mandrake' = a small plant with forked roots like legs; 'manned with an agate' = served by a jewel on which small figures are carved).

lines 14–22 Humour at Prince Hal's expense: he doesn't yet shave ('not yet fledge'); his face may be princely ('face-royal' = a ten shilling coin stamped with a royal head), but a barber cannot earn six pence by shaving the prince, because he has no face hair – and yet he calls himself a man ('writ man')!

---

**water** urine
**party that owed it** person who produced it
**moe** more
**gird at** mock, jeer
**litter** young pigs
**set me off** make a comical contrast

**whoreson** abominable
**vile apparel** ragged clothes
**juvenal** juvenile
**crowing** laughing boastfully
**slops** baggy breeches
**band** bond, security

# ACT 1 SCENE 2
## London: a street

Enter Sir John FALSTAFF, with his PAGE bearing his sword and
buckler

FALSTAFF  Sirrah, you giant, what says the doctor to my water?

PAGE  He said, sir, the water itself was a good healthy water, but for the
party that owed it, he might have moe diseases than he knew for.

FALSTAFF  Men of all sorts take a pride to gird at me: the brain of this
foolish compounded clay-man is not able to invent anything that      5
intends to laughter more than I invent, or is invented on me; I am
not only witty in myself, but the cause that wit is in other men. I
do here walk before thee like a sow that hath overwhelmed all her
litter but one; if the prince put thee into my service for any other
reason than to set me off, why then I have no judgement. Thou       10
whoreson mandrake, thou art fitter to be worn in my cap, than to
wait at my heels. I was never manned with an agate till now, but
I will inset you neither in gold nor silver, but in vile apparel, and
send you back again to your master for a jewel – the juvenal the
prince your master, whose chin is not yet fledge; I will sooner have  15
a beard grow in the palm of my hand, than he shall get one off his
cheek, and yet he will not stick to say his face is a face royal: God
may finish it when He will, 'tis not a hair amiss yet: he may keep
it still at a face-royal, for a barber shall never earn sixpence out of
it; and yet he'll be crowing as if he had writ man ever since his    20
father was a bachelor. He may keep his own grace, but he's almost
out of mine, I can assure him. What said Master Dommelton
about the satin for my short cloak and my slops?

PAGE  He said, sir, you should procure him better assurance than Bardolph:
he would not take his band and yours, he liked not the security.     25

*Falstaff mockingly curses the tailor for refusing him credit, and implies
that the tailor's wife is unfaithful. He jokes about Bardolph, then tries to
avoid the Lord Chief Justice by pretending his servant is a beggar.*

## 1 Mocking the tailor, Bardolph and the servant

Use the following to help you explore how to speak Falstaff's lines.
The Page reports that Falstaff's tailor has refused to give him credit,
and wants 'security' before he will supply anything. Falstaff plays with
the word 'security' as he mocks the tailor. He goes on to mock
Bardolph and the servant of the Lord Chief Justice.

lines 26–7 In the Bible 'the glutton' was the rich man Dives who
was sent to Hell and asked for water to cool his tongue.
'Achitophel' was a traitor who rebelled against King David.

lines 29–30 Falstaff likens the tailor to a Puritan tradesman with
close-cropped hair, who tries to appear important by wearing high
heeled shoes and carrying bunches of keys on his belt.

lines 35–7 Cuckolds (deceived husbands) were supposed to wear
horns. Falstaff also puns on 'lightness', which could mean
unfaithfulness.

lines 38–41 In Shakespeare's time, a popular proverb about three
places with a bad reputation was: 'A man must not make choice of
a wife in Westminster, a servant in Paul's or a horse in Smithfield,
lest he choose a queen (prostitute), a knave, or a jade (broken-
down horse).' Servants often stood in the nave of St Paul's
Cathedral, waiting to be hired.

lines 42–62 The Lord Chief Justice once sent Prince Hal to
prison for striking him ('committed the Prince'). Falstaff banters
with the Justice's servant, using deafness and pretending to
mistake the servant's identity as tactics to avoid serious
discussion.

---

**bear ... hand** encourage me with
  hopes
**taking up** borrowing on credit
**as lief** as willingly
**ratsbane** poison
**horn of abundance** cornucopia,
  ever flowing with riches

**lanthorn** lantern
**stews** brothels
**robbery** the Gad's Hill robbery (in
  *Henry IV Part 1*)
**done good service** fought well
**with some charge** as a
  commander

FALSTAFF  Let him be damned like the glutton, pray God his tongue be
hotter, a whoreson Achitophel! a rascal, yea forsooth, knave, to bear
a gentleman in hand, and then stand upon security! The whoreson
smoothy-pates do now wear nothing but high shoes and bunches of
keys at their girdles, and if a man is through with them in honest        30
taking up, then they must stand upon security. I had as lief they
would put ratsbane in my mouth, as offer to stop it with security.
I looked a should have sent me two-and-twenty yards of satin, as I
am a true knight, and he sends me 'security'! Well he may sleep in
security, for he hath the horn of abundance, and the lightness of his     35
wife shines through it – Where's Bardolph? – and yet cannot he see,
though he have his own lanthorn to light him.

PAGE  He's gone in Smithfield to buy your worship a horse.

FALSTAFF  I bought him in Paul's, and he'll buy me a horse in
Smithfield: and I could get me but a wife in the stews, I were          40
manned, horsed and wived.

*Enter* LORD CHIEF JUSTICE *and* SERVANT

PAGE  Sir, here comes the nobleman that committed the prince for
striking him about Bardolph.

FALSTAFF  Wait close, I will not see him.

JUSTICE  What's he that goes there?                                       45

SERVANT  Falstaff, and't please your lordship.

JUSTICE  He that was in question for the robbery?

SERVANT  He, my lord; but he hath since done good service at
Shrewsbury, and, as I hear, is now going with some charge to the
Lord John of Lancaster.                                                   50

JUSTICE  What, to York? Call him back again.

SERVANT  Sir John Falstaff.

FALSTAFF  Boy, tell him I am deaf.

PAGE  You must speak louder, my master is deaf.

JUSTICE  I am sure he is, to the hearing of anything good. Go pluck him   55
by the elbow, I must speak with him.

SERVANT  Sir John!

FALSTAFF  What? A young knave and begging? Is there not wars? Is
there not employment? Doth not the king lack subjects? Do not
the rebels need soldiers? Though it be a shame to be on any side        60
but one, it is worse shame to beg than to be on the worst side, were
it worse than the name of Rebellion can tell how to make it.

*Falstaff insults and dismisses the servant, then ambiguously flatters the
Lord Chief Justice. He uses all kinds of tricks to avoid giving direct
answers to the Justice, who delivers a thinly veiled threat.*

## 1 Comic evasion (in pairs)

The Lord Chief Justice wants to know why Falstaff, suspected of being
involved in a robbery at Gad's Hill (in *Henry IV Part 1*, Act 2 Scene 2),
never came to see him. Falstaff does not wish to be called to account,
and talks about other things to evade being questioned.

Take parts as Falstaff and the Lord Chief Justice and speak lines 74–
178. In your first reading it is probably best not to pause to work out
language you do not understand.

Remember that Falstaff often pretends to be polite, but mockery and
insults lie behind his words. After your reading, talk together about all
the devices that Falstaff uses to avoid any serious examination of his
activities.

line 81 'your expedition to Shrewsbury' – In *Part 1*, Falstaff led a
company of soldiers who were nearly all killed at the battle of
Shrewsbury. Falstaff falsely claimed to have killed Hotspur in the
battle.

lines 82–3 'his majesty is returned with some discomfort from
Wales' – King Henry IV, after the battle of Shrewsbury, led an
expedition against the Welsh.

line 88 'lethargy' (slowness of movement) – King Henry may
have suffered from syphilis, a sexually transmitted disease.
Falstaff may be punning on 'lechery'.

line 93 'Galen' – Falstaff often pretends to be well-read. Galen
was a famous Greek physician of the second century AD whose
writings were much studied in Elizabethan times.

---

**hunt counter** follow the wrong
  scent, are mistaken
**avaunt!** clear off!
**abroad** out of doors
**advice** doctor's orders

**smack of an ague** appearance of
  sickness
**saltness of time** dryness of old age
**it original** its cause
**marking** hearing, attending
**by the heels** in the stocks

SERVANT  You mistake me, sir.

FALSTAFF  Why, sir, did I say you were an honest man? Setting my
    knighthood and my soldiership aside, I had lied in my throat if I   65
    had said so.

SERVANT  I pray you, sir, then set your knighthood and your soldiership
    aside, and give me leave to tell you, you lie in your throat, if you
    say I am any other than an honest man.

FALSTAFF  I give thee leave to tell me? So I lay aside that which grows   70
    to me! If thou gettest any leave of me, hang me; if thou takest leave,
    thou wert better be hanged, you hunt counter: hence, avaunt!

SERVANT  Sir, my lord would speak with you.

JUSTICE  Sir John Falstaff, a word with you.

FALSTAFF  My good lord, God give your lordship good time of day. I am   75
    glad to see your lordship abroad, I heard say your lordship was sick.
    I hope your lordship goes abroad by advice. Your lordship, though
    not clean past your youth, have yet some smack of an ague in you,
    some relish of the saltness of time in you, and I most humbly
    beseech your lordship to have a reverend care of your health.   80

JUSTICE  Sir John, I sent for you before your expedition to Shrewsbury.

FALSTAFF  And't please your lordship, I hear his majesty is returned
    with some discomfort from Wales.

JUSTICE  I talk not of his majesty: you would not come when I sent for you.

FALSTAFF  And I hear moreover, his highness is fallen into this same   85
    whoreson apoplexy.

JUSTICE  Well, God mend him. I pray you let me speak with you.

FALSTAFF  This apoplexy, as I take it, is a kind of lethargy, and't please
    your lordship, a kind of sleeping in the blood, a whoreson tingling.

JUSTICE  What tell you me of it? Be it as it is.   90

FALSTAFF  It hath it original from much grief, from study and
    perturbation of the brain. I have read the cause of his effects in
    Galen, it is a kind of deafness.

JUSTICE  I think you are fallen into the disease, for you hear not what
    I say to you.   95

FALSTAFF  Very well, my lord, very well. Rather and't please you, it is
    the disease of not listening, the malady of not marking, that I am
    troubled withal.

JUSTICE  To punish you by the heels, would amend the attention of
    your ears, and I care not if I do become your physician.   100

*Falstaff uses puns and other tricks of language to shield himself from the Justice's criticisms. He claims that the times do not value the valour and intelligence of young men like himself.*

## 1 Serious and comic (in pairs)

Carry on speaking lines 74–178 as Falstaff and the Lord Chief Justice. Experiment with ways in which Falstaff varies his tone and style as he invents new ways of deflecting the Lord Chief Justice's criticism. Remember that Falstaff is never fully serious and turns as many of his replies as possible into humour.

lines 101–4 Falstaff's response to the Lord Chief Justice's warning that he will become Falstaff's physician, is to pun on 'patient'. In the Bible, Job suffered many afflictions with great patience. By 'make some dram of a scruple' Falstaff means feel a scrap of doubt (drams and scruples were tiny units of weight).

lines 107–8 Military service ('land-service') would excuse him from reporting to the Lord Chief Justice.

line 110 Falstaff pretends to mistake 'infamy' (disrepute) for 'clothing'.

lines 115–16 The famous Shakespeare critic Dr Samuel Johnson wrote: 'I do not understand this joke.' Neither does anyone else, so make your own guess.

lines 128–9 Falstaff puns on 'gravity' (seriousness) and 'gravy' (sweat).

line 131–2 An angel was a gold coin. Traders often weighed it to ensure it had not had pieces cut off.

line 134 A costermonger is a seller of apples. Falstaff implies that only money matters these days.

---

**loath to gall** reluctant to hurt
**gilded over** glowingly covered up
**quiet o'er-posting** escaping
 unpunished
**wassail candle** very large candle
**tallow** animal fat, dripping

**bearherd** keeper of performing
 bears
**pregnancy** quick-wittedness
**reckonings** tavern bills
**vaward** vanguard
**wags** jokers

FALSTAFF I am as poor as Job, my lord, but not so patient: your lordship may minister the potion of imprisonment to me in respect of poverty, but how I shall be your patient to follow your prescriptions, the wise may make some dram of a scruple, or indeed a scruple itself.

JUSTICE I sent for you when there were matters against you for your 105 life to come speak with me.

FALSTAFF As I was then advised by my learned counsel in the laws of this land-service, I did not come.

JUSTICE Well, the truth is, Sir John, you live in great infamy.

FALSTAFF He that buckles himself in my belt cannot live in less. 110

JUSTICE Your means are very slender and your waste is great.

FALSTAFF I would it were otherwise, I would my means were greater and my waist slender.

JUSTICE You have misled the youthful prince.

FALSTAFF The young prince hath misled me. I am the fellow with the 115 great belly, and he my dog.

JUSTICE Well, I am loath to gall a new-healed wound: your day's service at Shrewsbury hath a little gilded over your night's exploit on Gad's Hill. You may thank th'unquiet time for your quiet o'er-posting that action. 120

FALSTAFF My lord?

JUSTICE But since all is well, keep it so: wake not a sleeping wolf.

FALSTAFF To wake a wolf is as bad as smell a fox.

JUSTICE What? You are as a candle, the better part burnt out.

FALSTAFF A wassail candle, my lord, all tallow – if I did say of wax, my 125 growth would approve the truth.

JUSTICE There is not a white hair in your fac , but should have his effect of gravity.

FALSTAFF His effect of gravy, gravy, gravy.

JUSTICE You follow the young prince up and down, like his ill angel. 130

FALSTAFF Not so, my lord, your ill angel is light, but I hope he that looks upon me will take me without weighing; and yet in some respects I grant I cannot go. I cannot tell: virtue is of so little regard in these costermongers' times, that true valour is turned bearherd, pregnancy is made a tapster, and his quick wit wasted in giving 135 reckonings; all the other gifts appertinent to man, as the malice of this age shapes them, are not worth a gooseberry. You that are old consider not the capacities of us that are young: you do measure the heat of our livers with the bitterness of your galls; and we that are in the vaward of our youth, I must confess, are wags too. 140

*The Justice mocks Falstaff's claim to be young. Falstaff is unabashed and continues to joke, claiming that his great bravery is exploited by the English who continually rely on his fighting prowess.*

What line opposite is Falstaff (right) saying to the Lord Chief Justice?

## 1 Falstaff's appearance (in pairs)

In lines 142–6, the Lord Chief Justice describes Falstaff's physical appearance. As one person slowly speaks the lines, the other, as Falstaff, reacts to each item of the description.

## 2 Puns are catching!

The Lord Chief Justice leaves with a pun of his own; 'bear crosses' could mean 'endure afflictions' or 'save money' (silver coins were stamped with a cross on one side). Invent a gesture for the Justice to help the audience understand the pun.

---

**scroll** list
**hallooing** hunting cries
**caper with me** compete with me in dancing
**box of th'ear** see page 166
**ashes and sackcloth** traditional signs of mourning

**sack** Spanish white wine
**severed** parted (from Prince Hal)
**spit white** be healthy
**dangerous action** hot battle
**peep out his head** happen
**furnish me forth** equip my troops

JUSTICE  Do you set down your name in the scroll of youth, that are
written down old with all the characters of age? Have you not a moist
eye, a dry hand, a yellow cheek, a white beard, a decreasing leg, an
increasing belly? Is not your voice broken, your wind short, your
chin double, your wit single, and every part about you blasted with       145
antiquity? And will you yet call yourself young? Fie, fie, fie, Sir John.
FALSTAFF  My lord, I was born about three of the clock in the afternoon,
with a white head, and something a round belly. For my voice, I have
lost it with hallooing, and singing of anthems. To approve my youth
further, I will not: the truth is, I am only old in judgement and          150
understanding; and he that will caper with me for a thousand marks,
let him lend me the money and have at him. For the box of th'ear that
the prince gave you, he gave it like a rude prince, and you took it like
a sensible lord. I have checked him for it, and the young lion repents
– marry, not in ashes and sackcloth, but in new silk and old sack.        155
JUSTICE  Well, God send the prince a better companion.
FALSTAFF  God send the companion a better prince. I cannot rid my
hands of him.
JUSTICE  Well, the king hath severed you: I hear you are going with
Lord John of Lancaster against the Archbishop and the Earl of             160
Northumberland.
FALSTAFF  Yea, I thank your pretty sweet wit for it; but look you pray,
all you that kiss my Lady Peace at home, that our armies join not
in a hot day: for, by the Lord, I take but two shirts out with me,
and I mean not to sweat extraordinarily; if it be a hot day, and I        165
brandish anything but a bottle, I would I might never spit white
again: there is not a dangerous action can peep out his head, but
I am thrust upon it. Well, I cannot last ever, but it was alway yet
the trick of our English nation, if they have a good thing to make
it too common. If ye will needs say I am an old man, you should           170
give me rest; I would to God my name were not so terrible to the
enemy as it is: I were better to be eaten to death with a rust, than
to be scoured to nothing with perpetual motion.
JUSTICE  Well, be honest, be honest, and God bless your expedition.
FALSTAFF  Will your lordship lend me a thousand pound to furnish me       175
forth?
JUSTICE  Not a penny, not a penny: you are too impatient to bear
crosses. Fare you well. Commend me to my cousin Westmoreland.

[*Exeunt Lord Chief Justice and Servant*]

*Falstaff reflects that love of money and sex, and the problems they bring, are simply part of life. He sends letters, and says he can turn anything to advantage. The rebels begin a council of war.*

## 1 Falstaff's technique

Falstaff reveals more of his style. He uses polite language (with veiled insults) to a superior's face, but behind their back he speaks as he feels. The Lord Chief Justice asks Falstaff to carry a message to Westmoreland, but after the Justice has left, Falstaff speaks his mind: If I do, strike me ('fillip me') with a sledgehammer ('beetle') that is so heavy that it takes three men to lift.

Images of disease run through the play, and in lines 186–7 Falstaff turns his lack of money into an incurable disease. As he leaves the stage Falstaff claims he will ensure that diseases bring him profit. He can even make use of his limp ('halt') that is caused by a sexually transmitted disease ('pox') to obtain a higher pension.

Falstaff's lines 194–5 are another clue to his character and use of language: 'A good wit will make use of anything.' Look back through the scene and identify some of the things that Falstaff's wit turns to his own advantage, beginning with his Page, his tailor and Bardolph, and ending with his limp.

You will find more help with how Falstaff uses language on pages 20–6, and on page 201.

## 2 Planning the rebellion (in groups of four)

Take parts and speak Scene 3. Try to gain a first impression of each man's attitude to the proposed rebellion. Then work on the activities on pages 32, 34 and 36.

---

**covetousness** greedy desire for other people's wealth
**a can part** he can separate
**galls** irritates
**the degrees** facts of human nature
**prevent** turn away
**groat** silver coin worth four pence

**consumption** wasting illness
**colour** pretext, excuse
**commodity** self-interest, profit
**allow the occasion** approve the cause
**puissance** strength, mighty army

FALSTAFF  If I do, fillip me with a three-man beetle. A man can no more
    separate age and covetousness than a can part young limbs and      180
    lechery; but the gout galls the one, and the pox pinches the other,
    and so both the degrees prevent my curses. Boy!
PAGE  Sir.
FALSTAFF  What money is in my purse?
PAGE  Seven groats and two pence.      185
FALSTAFF  I can get no remedy against this consumption of the purse:
    borrowing only lingers and lingers it out, but the disease is incurable.
    Go bear this letter to my lord of Lancaster, this to the prince, this to
    the Earl of Westmoreland, and this to old Mistress Ursula, whom I
    have weekly sworn to marry since I perceived the first white hair of      190
    my chin. About it, you know where to find me. A pox of this gout, or
    a gout of this pox, for the one or the other plays the rogue with my
    great toe. 'Tis no matter if I do halt: I have the wars for my colour,
    and my pension shall seem the more reasonable. A good wit will
    make use of anything: I will turn diseases to commodity.      195

*Exeunt*

# ACT 1    SCENE 3
## York: the Archbishop's Palace

Enter the ARCHBISHOP of York, THOMAS MOWBRAY (Earl Marshal),
the LORD HASTINGS, and LORD BARDOLPH

ARCHBISHOP  Thus have you heard our cause and known our means,
    And, my most noble friends, I pray you all
    Speak plainly your opinions of our hopes,
    And first, Lord Marshal, what say you to it?
MOWBRAY  I well allow the occasion of our arms,      5
    But gladly would be better satisfied
    How in our means we should advance ourselves
    To look with forehead bold and big enough
    Upon the power and puissance of the king.

*Hastings hopes that reinforcements from Northumberland will enlarge the rebel army. Lord Bardolph and the Archbishop recall that Hotspur's defeated army was too small. Bardolph advises caution.*

## 1 Caution before hope

Hastings reports the size of the rebel army ('musters', 'file') and hopes for reinforcements ('supplies') from Northumberland. Lord Bardolph favours waiting until the reinforcing troops join the rebels. He is all too aware that rumours of weakness may spread if Northumberland's soldiers are not seen to arrive. The rebels remind themselves that a major reason for Hotspur's defeat at Shrewsbury was that the reinforcements he expected did not arrive.

a  Compare Lord Bardolph's line 23 (describing rumours) with Rumour's lines 15–16 in the Induction.

b  Most people find Lord Bardolph's lines 36–41 difficult to interpret. Many believe that one or more lines that Shakespeare wrote are missing. Check if you agree that the general sense is: 'Even if our present military action is based on hope, it is like the hope of seeing buds in Spring time, when it is more likely they will be killed by frost.'

## 2 Shakespeare's personal experience? (in pairs)

In 1597, Shakespeare bought New Place, the largest house in Stratford-upon-Avon. Some people believe that lines 41–62 arise from Shakespeare's plans for some rebuilding of the house ('model' is an architect's plan, 'offices' are rooms). Others argue that the lines are inspired by three verses in the Bible, Luke 14.28–30. Luke's parable of the builder advises careful calculation before beginning to build.

Explore ways of speaking Lord Bardolph's lines to make them as persuasive as possible.

---

**men of choice**  picked soldiers
**hold up head**  be a sufficiently
  large army
**marry**  by the Virgin Mary
  (a mild oath)
**aids incertain**  doubtful
  reinforcements

**lined**  strengthened
**project of a power**  an army
**winking**  blindly
**lay down likelihoods**  consider
  possibilities
**on foot**  moving forward
**great work**  rebellion

HASTINGS  Our present musters grow upon the file                                        10
          To five-and-twenty thousand men of choice,
          And our supplies live largely in the hope
          Of great Northumberland, whose bosom burns
          With an incensèd fire of injuries.
LORD BARDOLPH  The question then, Lord Hastings, standeth thus:      15
          Whether our present five-and-twenty thousand
          May hold up head without Northumberland.
HASTINGS  With him we may.
LORD BARDOLPH                 Yea marry, there's the point;
          But if without him we be thought too feeble,
          My judgement is we should not step too far                               20
          Till we have his assistance by the hand;
          For in a theme so bloody-faced as this,
          Conjecture, expectation, and surmise
          Of aids incertain, should not be admitted.
ARCHBISHOP  'Tis very true, Lord Bardolph, for indeed                       25
          It was young Hotspur's cause at Shrewsbury.
LORD BARDOLPH  It was, my lord; who lined himself with hope,
          Eating the air, and promise of supply,
          Flatt'ring himself in project of a power
          Much smaller than the smallest of his thoughts,                       30
          And so with great imagination,
          Proper to madmen, led his powers to death,
          And, winking, leaped into destruction.
HASTINGS  But, by your leave, it never yet did hurt
          To lay down likelihoods and forms of hope.                            35
LORD BARDOLPH  Yes, if this present quality of war –
          Indeed the instant action, a cause on foot –
          Lives so in hope, as in an early spring
          We see th'appearing buds, which to prove fruit
          Hope gives not so much warrant as despair                             40
          That frosts will bite them. When we mean to build,
          We first survey the plot, then draw the model,
          And when we see the figure of the house,
          Then must we rate the cost of the erection,
          Which if we find outweighs ability,                                        45
          What do we then, but draw anew the model
          In fewer offices, or at least desist
          To build at all? Much more in this great work

*Lord Bardolph argues that the rebels should carefully consider whether they have sufficient soldiers. Hastings says they have, because King Henry fights on three fronts against the Welsh, the French and the rebels.*

## 1 Planning for success

Lord Bardolph compares how careful people plan and build a house with how the rebels should carry out the rebellion. If they do not have enough soldiers, then their rebellion will fail, like a house builder with insufficient resources who is forced to abandon his half-built house ('part created cost').

Lord Bardolph's speech offers the actor many opportunities to accompany his words with actions (in one production he illustrated his argument by sketching on a large sheet of paper which he crumpled up and threw away at 'waste' in line 62). Invent your own actions to accompany Bardolph's lines 41–62.

## 2 Where and who?

Step into role as Hastings and speak his lines 69–85. Use the map on page 2 (or your own copy of the map) to point to as you try to persuade the other rebels that they have sufficient soldiers to defeat King Henry. Also find ways (for example, by accent or gesture) of signifying the persons you name:

Glendower: Leader of the Welsh forces (appears in *Part 1*).

The Duke of Lancaster: Prince John, Prince Hal's brother.

Westmoreland: Second-in-command of Prince John's army.

Harry Monmouth: Prince Hal (who was born at Monmouth).

---

**model** plan, design
**estate** wealth, strength
**his opposite** our opponents
**fortify in paper** have only paper soldiers
**utmost man** maximum number of soldiers

**divisions** military forces
**as the times do brawl** in these turbulent days
**heads** armies
**coffers** treasure chests
**Baying him at the heels** barking at his back

(Which is almost to pluck a kingdom down
And set another up) should we survey 50
The plot of situation and the model,
Consent upon a sure foundation,
Question surveyors, know our own estate,
How able such a work to undergo,
To weigh against his opposite; or else 55
We fortify in paper, and in figures,
Using the names of men instead of men,
Like one that draws the model of an house
Beyond his power to build it; who, half through,
Gives o'er, and leaves his part created cost 60
A naked subject to the weeping clouds,
And waste for churlish winter's tyranny.

HASTINGS  Grant that our hopes, yet likely of fair birth,
Should be still-born, and that we now possessed
The utmost man of expectation: 65
I think we are a body strong enough,
Even as we are, to equal with the king.

LORD BARDOLPH  What, is the king but five-and-twenty thousand?

HASTINGS  To us no more, nay not so much, Lord Bardolph,
For his divisions, as the times do brawl, 70
Are in three heads: one power against the French,
And one against Glendower; perforce a third
Must take up us. So is the infirm king
In three divided, and his coffers sound
With hollow poverty and emptiness. 75

ARCHBISHOP  That he should draw his several strengths together
And come against us in full puissance
Need not to be dreaded.

HASTINGS                                   If he should do so,
He leaves his back unarmed, the French and Welsh
Baying him at the heels: never fear that. 80

LORD BARDOLPH  Who is it like should lead his forces hither?

HASTINGS  The Duke of Lancaster and Westmoreland;
Against the Welsh, himself and Harry Monmouth;
But who is substituted against the French
I have no certain notice.

*The Archbishop criticises the common people of England for their
fickleness: they now hate King Henry when once they welcomed him,
and love the late King Richard whom they once despised.*

## 1 Publicity campaign

The Archbishop decides on a widespread proclamation of the rebels'
reasons for their armed insurrection against King Henry ('publish the
occasion of our arms'). In medieval times, there were none of the
modern ways of spreading information (television, newspapers and so
on). It is probable that a handbill would be prepared to be nailed up in
towns and villages. Most people could not read, so a simple message
that one person could read aloud was required.

Design the handbill or poster giving the rebels' reasons. Use the
information on pages 1 and 112 to help you.

## 2 Ordinary people (in pairs)

The Archbishop is thinking of the events that Shakespeare dramatises
in *Richard II*. Bullingbrook (who became Henry IV) was welcomed by
the ordinary people, and King Richard was reviled by them.

The Archbishop is contemptuous of the ordinary people of England
('The commonwealth'). He thinks that they cannot be trusted, and that
they all too easily changed their loyalty to King Richard and King Henry.

a Identify the different ways in which the Archbishop describes the
common people in lines 90, 91, 95 and 97.

b Speak his lines, putting distaste into your tone when you speak
words which refer to the people.

c Talk together about what you think his speech reveals about the
Archbishop, as a churchman, as a·politician, and as a rebel who
depends on popular support.

---

**surfeited** over-fed
**habitation** house, dwelling
**the vulgar heart** popular acclaim
**fond Many** foolish multitude
**trimmèd** dressed
**cast** vomit
**disgorge** vomit up

**glutton bosom** greedy body
**enamoured on** besotted with
**Past and to come** the past and
the future
**draw our numbers** assemble our
army

ARCHBISHOP                    Let us on,                                    85
    And publish the occasion of our arms.
    The commonwealth is sick of their own choice,
    Their over-greedy love hath surfeited:
    An habitation giddy and unsure
    Hath he that buildeth on the vulgar heart.                    90
    O thou fond Many, with what loud applause
    Didst thou beat heaven with blessing Bullingbrook,
    Before he was what thou wouldst have him be!
    And being now trimmèd in thine own desires,
    Thou, beastly feeder, art so full of him                      95
    That thou provok'st thyself to cast him up.
    So, so, thou common dog, didst thou disgorge
    Thy glutton bosom of the royal Richard,
    And now thou wouldst eat thy dead vomit up,
    And howl'st to find it. What trust is in these times?         100
    They, that when Richard lived would have him die,
    Are now become enamoured on his grave;
    Thou that threw'st dust upon his goodly head
    When through proud London he came sighing on
    After th'admired heels of Bullingbrook,                       105
    Criest now: 'O earth, yield us that king again
    And take thou this!' O thoughts of men accursed!
    Past and to come seems best; things present, worst.
MOWBRAY  Shall we go draw our numbers, and set on?
HASTINGS  We are Time's subjects, and Time bids be gone.          110

*Exeunt*

37

# Looking back at Act 1

*Activities for groups or individuals*

'Enter RUMOUR, painted full of tongues.' Rumour's opening speech creates a sense of uncertainty, disorder and treachery that will pervade the whole play. Design your own version of Rumour's costume.

## 1 Spread a rumour!

Improvise a short scene showing how rumours spread today by word of mouth, by television, and by radio.

## 2 Scene locations

In this edition, locations are given for each scene, but no one really knows for certain precisely where Shakespeare intended every scene to be set. On the open Elizabethan stage there were no elaborate sets. One scene flowed quickly into the next. In the modern theatre there is usually a set design that can be speedily changed to show the audience a different location. Design a simple set that can swiftly change to show the three different locations in Act 1.

## 3 Rumours of war

Newspapers did not exist in Henry's time (or in Shakespeare's). But imagine they did, and that you are a reporter who interviews everyone who appears in Scenes 1 and 3. Write your story under a compelling headline.

## 4 'Let Order die'

In Scene 1, Northumberland's fiery cry for disorder to reign in England expresses a major theme – order and disorder – which will run through the play. In every following scene Shakespeare balances civil order against the prospect of rebellion and chaos. Find a way of vividly expressing how the theme appears in each scene in Act 1 (for example, in three tableaux, or cartoons, or quotation collages, and so on).

## 5 Time

The act ends with Hastings' 'We are Time's subjects, and Time bids be gone.' A major theme of *Part 2* is 'Time' (see page 190). Suggest how the final speech in both Scenes 1 and 2 also embody the theme of time.

## 6 Dramatic construction

Shakespeare structures the play to ensure that each scene contains ironic and dramatic contrasts with its neighbouring scenes. He alternates 'serious' and 'comic' scenes so that the comic subplot mirrors or inverts the main political plot in some way.

In the first two scenes, Northumberland's sickness finds an ironic echo in Falstaff's diseases. The rebels' hasty preparations for war contrast with Falstaff's long leisurely complaint against his tailor. Identify a few more ways in which Scene 2 adds to the meaning and dramatic impact of Scenes 1 and 3. As you read on, look out for further examples of how neighbouring scenes deepen each other's effect.

*The Hostess wants Falstaff arrested, but warns the constables that he is
dangerous. She tells them that Falstaff owes her money, and suggests
where he might be in London. Falstaff approaches.*

## 1 Comic business (in groups of five)

Shakespeare took delight in inventing comic constables. Sergeant Fang
and Constable ('yeoman') Snare are only tiny roles, but most productions
of the play try to make their performances as funny as possible.
Mistress Quickly, the Hostess of the tavern, adds to the fun because
her language is a riot of malapropisms (mistaken words) and double
meanings, usually sexual.

Take parts (Hostess, Fang, Snare, Falstaff, Page) and rehearse lines
1–46 showing the attempted arrest of Falstaff. Use the following, and
Activity 1 on page 42, to help your preparation:

• Invent as much comic business as you can for the two constables.
  In Shakespeare's time, Snare was probably played by a tall thin
  actor, and entered at line 4 behind Fang who cannot see him.

• In Elizabethan London, 'a' was the colloquial form of 'he', as in
  lines 3, 11, 16 and 19.

• The Hostess (acted by a boy in Shakespeare's time, see page 60) is
  often played as being completely unaware of the sexual
  implications of much of what she says: 'stand', 'entered', 'stab',
  'weapon', 'foin' (thrust), and so on. But she does know that Pie
  Corner not only sells saddles, but is also notorious for prostitutes,
  so she apologises for mentioning it: 'saving your manhoods'.

She often repeats herself and loves to use long or impressive
words, but usually muddles them up ('infinitive' for 'infinite',
'continuantly' for 'incontinently', 'indited' for 'invited', 'exion' for
'action', and so on).

---

**entered the action** written down
  the law suit
**a stand to't?** he do it? (his duty)
**close** grapple
**warrant** assure
**upon my score** in my debt
**Lubber's/Lumbert** Leopard's/
  Lombard

**A hundred mark** £66
**long one** huge amount
**borne** waited
**arrant malmsey-nose** notorious
  red-nosed drunkard
**offices** duties

# London: the Boar's Head Tavern

*Enter* HOSTESS *of the tavern, and an officer,* FANG,
*followed by yeoman* SNARE

HOSTESS  Master Fang, have you entered the action?
FANG  It is entered.
HOSTESS  Where's your yeoman? Is't a lusty yeoman? Will a stand to't?
FANG  Sirrah – Where's Snare?
HOSTESS  O Lord, ay, good Master Snare.                                    5
SNARE  Here, here.
FANG  Snare, we must arrest Sir John Falstaff.
HOSTESS  Yea, good Master Snare, I have entered him and all.
SNARE  It may chance cost some of us our lives, for he will stab.
HOSTESS  Alas the day, take heed of him: he stabbed me in mine own      10
    house, most beastly, in good faith. A cares not what mischief he
    does: if his weapon be out, he will foin like any devil, he will spare
    neither man, woman, nor child.
FANG  If I can close with him, I care not for his thrust.
HOSTESS  No, nor I neither, I'll be at your elbow.                        15
FANG  And I but fist him once, and a come but within my view –
HOSTESS  I am undone by his going. I warrant you, he's an infinitive thing
    upon my score. Good Master Fang, hold him sure; good Master
    Snare, let him not 'scape. A comes continuantly to Pie Corner –
    saving your manhoods – to buy a saddle, and he is indited to dinner   20
    to the Lubber's Head in Lumbert Street to Master Smooth's the
    silkman. I pray you since my exion is entered, and my case so openly
    known to the world, let him be brought in to his answer. A hundred
    mark is a long one for a poor lone woman to bear, and I have borne,
    and borne, and borne, and have been fubbed off, and fubbed off, and   25
    fubbed off, from this day to that day, that it is a shame to be thought
    on. There is no honesty in such dealing, unless a woman should be
    made an ass, and a beast, to bear every knave's wrong. – Yonder he
    comes, and that arrant malmsey-nose knave Bardolph with him. Do
    your offices, do your offices, Master Fang and Master Snare, do me,   30
    do me, do me your offices.

*The officers try to arrest Falstaff, but he resists. Confusion reigns, but the Lord Chief Justice restores order and rebukes Falstaff. The Hostess explains her grievance.*

## 1 An attempted arrest (in small groups)

The following can help you stage the comic action in lines 32–46.

- The Hostess is enraged that Falstaff orders Bardolph to kill Fang. Her repetitions and malapropisms add to the confusion. She wants to call Falstaff 'homicidal', but uses 'honeysuckle', 'honeyseed' and 'hempseed' instead.

- The officers shout 'A rescue', which was the cry of constables when someone tried to drag away an arrested man. But the Hostess misunderstands, and she calls the bystanders to help with a rescue.

- The tiny Page adds to the confusion, shouting a string of insulting nonsense words, and a popular saying of the time: 'I'll tickle your catastrophe!' In some productions he adds actions to his words, and dances around the Hostess beating her behind.

## 2 Enter the Lord Chief Justice

The Lord Chief Justice imposes order on the chaos that the attempted arrest of Falstaff has created. As you read on, keep in mind how the Falstaff subplot reflects the political theme of order and disorder in the main plot of the play (see pages 39 and 191).

## 3 Everyday English

'Eaten me out of house and home' (line 57) is a commonplace saying today. Suggest one or two reasons why this saying has survived unchanged for over 400 years, whereas 'whose mare's dead?' ('what's all the fuss?', line 32) has dropped out of everyday use in the English language.

---

**at the suit** on the charge, request
**varlets** knaves
**quean** prostitute
**channel** gutter, open sewer
**queller** killer
**wot ta** know you

**hempseed** homicide, or hangman's hempen rope
**become your place** dignify your status
**substance** wealth
**mare** (line 59) nightmare

*Enter Sir John* [FALSTAFF] *and* BARDOLPH *and the* [PAGE-] boy

FALSTAFF  How now, whose mare's dead? What's the matter?

FANG  I arrest you at the suit of Mistress Quickly.

FALSTAFF   Away, varlets! Draw, Bardolph, cut me off the villain's
head, throw the quean in the channel.                                         35

HOSTESS  Throw me in the channel? I'll throw thee in the channel. Wilt
thou, wilt thou, thou bastardly rogue? Murder, murder! Ah, thou
honeysuckle villain, wilt thou kill God's officers, and the king's?
Ah, thou honeyseed rogue, thou art a honeyseed, a man-queller,
and a woman-queller.                                                          40

FALSTAFF  Keep them off, Bardolph.

OFFICERS  A rescue, a rescue!

HOSTESS  Good people, bring a rescue or two. Thou wot, wot thou,
thou wot, wot ta? Do, do, thou rogue! Do, thou hempseed!

PAGE  Away, you scullian, you rampallian, you fustilarian! I'll tickle        45
your catastrophe!

*Enter* LORD CHIEF JUSTICE *and his Men*

JUSTICE  What is the matter? Keep the peace here, ho!

HOSTESS  Good my lord, be good to me. I beseech you stand to me.

JUSTICE  How now, Sir John? What are you brawling here?
Doth this become your place, your time, and business?                        50
You should have been well on your way to York.
Stand from him, fellow, wherefore hang'st thou upon him?

HOSTESS  O my most worshipful lord, and't please your grace, I am a
poor widow of Eastcheap, and he is arrested at my suit.

JUSTICE  For what sum?                                                        55

HOSTESS  It is more than for some, my lord, it is for all – all I have; he
hath eaten me out of house and home, he hath put all my
substance into that fat belly of his; but I will have some of it out
again, or I will ride thee a-nights like the mare.

FALSTAFF  I think I am as like to ride the mare, if I have any vantage of     60
ground to get up.

JUSTICE  How comes this, Sir John? What man of good temper would
endure this tempest of exclamation? Are you not ashamed to
enforce a poor widow to so rough a course to come by her own?

FALSTAFF  What is the gross sum that I owe thee?                             65

*The Hostess gives precise particulars of Falstaff's promise to marry her.*
*Falstaff claims that poverty has driven her mad. He refuses to accept*
*the Justice's demand that he pay up.*

## 1 Play the Hostess (in pairs)

The Hostess' accusation of Falstaff (lines 66–80) is one of the famous
speeches of the play. Her very detailed description is like a parody of
a witness giving evidence at a trial. Explore different ways of speaking
the lines.

## 2 Why?

The Hostess claims that 'in Wheeson [Whitsun] week', Prince Hal
broke Falstaff's head for comparing his father, King Henry, to 'a
singing man of Windsor'. Scholars have argued endlessly over lines
69–70. Is it likely that the Prince would strike Falstaff for likening his
father to a singer? One suggestion is that the 'singing man' is a
claimant to the English throne.

Step into role as a Shakespeare expert and invent an explanation of
your own in a style that might convince other experts.

## 3 '… her eldest son is like you'

Falstaff manages to insult both the Hostess and the Lord Chief
Justice in lines 81–2. Advise the actor how he might deliver the lines.

## 4 How will Falstaff escape?

The Justice rebukes Falstaff and orders him, as his honour requires
('in th'effect of your reputation'), to pay the debt he owes the Hostess.
Falstaff defends himself vigorously and asks for release from arrest on
the grounds that he is on military service for the king. Before you turn
the page, make a guess at what Falstaff will do to get out of this tricky
situation.

---

**parcel-gilt** partly gilded
**Dolphin chamber** (inn room name)
**Keech** a roll of animal fat
**gossip** neighbour
**mess** drop
**green** fresh, unhealed

**book-oath** swearing on the Bible
**in good case** well off, prosperous
**confident brow** bold look
**level consideration** fair weighing of the facts
**sneap** rebuke
**suitor** beggar

HOSTESS  Marry, if thou wert an honest man, thyself and the money
too: thou didst swear to me upon a parcel-gilt goblet, sitting in my
Dolphin chamber at the round table by a sea-coal fire, upon
Wednesday in Wheeson week, when the prince broke thy head for
liking his father to a singing man of Windsor – thou didst swear to    70
me then, as I was washing thy wound, to marry me, and make me
my lady thy wife. Canst thou deny it? Did not goodwife Keech the
butcher's wife come in then and call me gossip Quickly, coming in
to borrow a mess of vinegar, telling us she had a good dish of
prawns, whereby thou didst desire to eat some, whereby I told      75
thee they were ill for a green wound? And didst thou not, when
she was gone downstairs, desire me to be no more so familiarity
with such poor people, saying that ere long they should call me
madam? And didst thou not kiss me, and bid me fetch thee thirty
shillings? I put thee now to thy book-oath, deny it if thou canst.     80

FALSTAFF  My lord, this is a poor mad soul, and she says up and down
the town that her eldest son is like you. She hath been in good
case, and the truth is poverty hath distracted her. But for these
foolish officers, I beseech you I may have redress against them.

JUSTICE  Sir John, Sir John, I am well acquainted with your manner of    85
wrenching the true cause the false way. It is not a confident brow,
nor the throng of words that come with such more than impudent
sauciness from you, can thrust me from a level consideration: you
have, as it appears to me, practised upon the easy-yielding spirit
of this woman, and made her serve your uses both in purse and in     90
person.

HOSTESS  Yea, in truth, my lord.

JUSTICE  Pray thee, peace. Pay her the debt you owe her, and unpay the
villainy you have done with her: the one you may do with sterling
money, and the other with current repentance.     95

FALSTAFF  My lord, I will not undergo this sneap without reply. You
call honourable boldness impudent sauciness: if a man will make
curtsy and say nothing, he is virtuous. No, my lord (my humble
duty remembered), I will not be your suitor. I say to you I do
desire deliverance from these officers, being upon hasty     100
employment in the king's affairs.

JUSTICE  You speak as having power to do wrong; but answer in
th'effect of your reputation, and satisfy the poor woman.

FALSTAFF  Come hither, hostess.

[*Takes her aside*]

*Gower brings news of military preparations.*
*Falstaff wins over the Hostess, and tells her to sell her possessions*
*in order to lend him more money.*

## 1 Falstaff charms the Hostess (in pairs)

Falstaff persuades the Hostess to drop her lawsuit against him and to
lend him more money. Lines 108–29 make a little scene on their own,
showing Falstaff at work to get his own way.

Take parts as Falstaff and the Hostess. Falstaff is all charm and
confidence, the Hostess is still reluctant but wants to be persuaded. To
help you:

a  Falstaff assures the Hostess that by pawning her plate (pewter
   tankards and plates) and her tapestries that cover the walls of the
   tavern's dining rooms, she will be at the front of fashion. She can
   replace them with glasses and painted cloths. Such items were
   very popular with the middle classes of Elizabethan England.
   They were a sign of prosperity and good taste. The painted cloths
   ('waterwork') would have different pictures: 'drollery' (comic
   scenes of Dutch life), the story of the prodigal son (from the
   Bible), or German hunting scenes.

b  'hook on': Falstaff instructs Bardolph to stick closely by the
   Hostess to ensure she gets the money.

c  Doll Tearsheet is a prostitute.

## 2 No reply

Notice how Falstaff's questions to the Lord Chief Justice receive no
reply. When you turn the page you will discover how Falstaff repays
the insult.

---

**fain** content, obliged
**bed-hangers** curtains around a
  four poster bed
**humours** moods
**draw the action** withdraw the
  lawsuit

**set on** encouraged by others
**twenty nobles** £6
**shift** arrangements
**foot** infantry
**horse** cavalry

*Enter [Master* GOWER *as] messenger*

JUSTICE  Now, Master Gower, what news?                    105
GOWER  The king, my lord, and Harry Prince of Wales
      Are near at hand; the rest the paper tells.

*[Gives a letter]*

FALSTAFF  As I am a gentleman!
HOSTESS  Faith, you said so before.
FALSTAFF  As I am a gentleman. Come, no more words of it.   110
HOSTESS  By this heavenly ground I tread on, I must be fain to pawn
      both my plate and the tapestry of my dining chambers.
FALSTAFF  Glasses, glasses, is the only drinking, and for thy walls a
      pretty slight drollery, or the story of the prodigal, or the German
      hunting in waterwork, is worth a thousand of these bed-hangers,   115
      and these fly-bitten tapestries. Let it be ten pounds, if thou canst.
      Come, and 'twere not for thy humours, there's not a better wench
      in England. Go wash thy face, and draw the action. Come, thou
      must not be in this humour with me, dost not know me? Come,
      come, I know thou wast set on to this.                   120
HOSTESS  Pray thee, Sir John, let it be but twenty nobles, i'faith I am
      loath to pawn my plate, so God save me, la.
FALSTAFF  Let it alone, I'll make other shift. You'll be a fool still.
HOSTESS  Well, you shall have it, though I pawn my gown. I hope you'll
      come to supper. You'll pay me all together?               125
FALSTAFF  Will I live? *[To Bardolph]* Go with her, with her, hook on,
      hook on.
HOSTESS  Will you have Doll Tearsheet meet you at supper?
FALSTAFF  No more words, let's have her.

*[Exeunt Hostess, Officers, Bardolph and Page]*

JUSTICE  I have heard better news.                          130
FALSTAFF  What's the news, my lord?
JUSTICE  Where lay the king tonight?
GOWER  At Basingstoke, my lord.
FALSTAFF  I hope, my lord, all's well. What is the news, my lord?
JUSTICE  Come all his forces back?                          135
GOWER  No, fifteen hundred foot, five hundred horse
      Are marched up to my lord of Lancaster
      Against Northumberland, and the Archbishop.
FALSTAFF  Comes the king back from Wales, my noble lord?

47

*Falstaff ignores the Lord Chief Justice, just as he had been ignored.*
*In Scene 2, Hal reflects on his weariness and low tastes. He says he is*
*disgraced by knowing Poins.*

## 1 Getting your own back (in groups of three)

Just as the Lord Chief Justice had ignored Falstaff's questions, so
Falstaff now ignores the Justice. His method is 'tap for tap', tit for tat,
paying back the insult in the same fashion. Take parts as Falstaff, the
Justice and Gower. Work out a performance of lines 130–53 to show
how Falstaff gives the Justice a dose of his own medicine.

## 2 Prince Hal (in pairs)

Prince Hal's conversation with Poins (lines 1–52) has been very
differently interpreted. Some critics claim that it shows he is full of
self-disgust at his association with the low-life company of the tavern.
Others claim he still enjoys it, and is just playing a part.

Take parts and speak lines 1–52. Don't pause to work out what you
do not understand, but after your first reading use the suggestions
below and on page 50 to help you:

- Hal says that his liking for weak beer and his association with
  Poins is really beneath him, tarnishing his status as a prince
  ('discolours the complexion of my greatness'). Do you think he
  really means it?

- In *Henry IV Part 1*, Hal and Poins were great friends, playing
  tricks on Falstaff. Now Hal says it is a disgrace for him to
  remember anything about Poins: his name, his clothing. As you
  read on, decide what you think are Hal's real feelings towards
  Poins. Also think about what Poins really feels about the prince.

---

**presently** very soon
**entreat** invite
**take soldiers up** recruit troops
**fencing grace** duelling style
**durst** dared
**attached** arrested
**vildly** vilely

**small beer** beer weakened with
water
**loosely studied** schooled in
villainy
**composition** mixture
**by my troth** truly
**superfluity** spare

JUSTICE  You shall have letters of me presently.                    140
        Come, go along with me, good master Gower.
FALSTAFF  My lord.
JUSTICE  What's the matter?
FALSTAFF  Master Gower, shall I entreat you with me at dinner?
GOWER  I must wait upon my good lord here, I thank you, good Sir John.   145
JUSTICE  Sir John, you loiter here too long, being you are to take
        soldiers up in counties as you go.
FALSTAFF  Will you sup with me, Master Gower?
JUSTICE  What foolish master taught you these manners, Sir John?
FALSTAFF  Master Gower, if they become me not, he was a fool that    150
        taught them me. This is the right fencing grace, my lord, tap for
        tap, and so part fair.
JUSTICE  Now the Lord lighten thee, thou art a great fool.

                                                    *Exeunt*


# ACT 2   SCENE 2
## London: Prince Hal's apartments

### Enter PRINCE HAL and POINS

PRINCE  Before God, I am exceeding weary.
POINS  Is't come to that? I had thought weariness durst not have
        attached one of so high a blood.
PRINCE  Faith, it does me, though it discolours the complexion of my
        greatness to acknowledge it: doth it not show vildly in me to desire   5
        small beer?
POINS  Why, a prince should not be so loosely studied as to remember
        so weak a composition.
PRINCE  Belike then my appetite was not princely got, for by my troth, I do
        now remember the poor creature small beer. But indeed these   10
        humble considerations make me out of love with my greatness. What
        a disgrace is it to me to remember thy name – or to know thy face
        tomorrow – or to take note how many pairs of silk stockings thou hast
        with these, and those that were the peach-coloured once – or to bear
        the inventory of thy shirts, as: one for superfluity, and another for use.   15

*Hal slanders Poins for his sexual misconduct. He says that he grieves inwardly for his father's sickness, but to show sadness would be hypocritical because of his disreputable life style.*

## 1 Hal's humour (in pairs)

Hal insults Poins in lines 16–22. Shakespeare's Elizabethan audience would probably enjoy the double meanings, but today neither the meaning nor the puns are immediately clear. For example, 'low countries' could mean the Netherlands, brothels or genitals, and 'holland' could be Holland or shirts of fine linen. Use the following summary to help you, then suggest how Hal might use accompanying actions and gestures to help audience understanding.

> 'When you have spare shirts, you play tennis, but you haven't played much for a long time because all your shirts have been used to make swaddling clothes for the babies you have fathered in the brothels. Your many children might go to heaven, because it is not their fault that they are illegitimate.'

## 2 Straight talking (in pairs)

Just how do Prince Hal and Poins speak to each other? Do they talk together as equals, or does Hal emphasise his superior status, and Poins his inferior social status? Poins says that he is a younger son ('second brother') and so has no inheritance, and in line 51 that he is handy with his fists (or light-fingered).

Experiment with ways of speaking all their dialogue to discover how far you think the prince and Poins reveal their true thoughts to each other. Do they use a joking tone, or one of veiled hostility and dislike, or some other tone? For example, just how does Poins speak 'I would think thee a most princely hypocrite' (line 41) and Hal speak 'And to thee' (line 48)?

---

**low ebb** shortage (low tide)
**inherit His kingdom** go to heaven
**kindreds** families
**stand the push** am ready for (from sword fencing)
**meet** appropriate
**Very hardly** with great difficulty

**the devil's book** the roll-call of Hell
**obduracy** moral corruption
**ostentation** outward show
**keeps the roadway** reflects public opinion
**accites** induces, causes
**engraffed** attached, grafted

But that the tennis-court-keeper knows better than I, for it is a low
ebb of linen with thee when thou keepest not racket there, as thou hast
not done a great while, because the rest of the low countries have
made a shift to eat up thy holland; and God knows whether those that
bawl out the ruins of thy linen shall inherit His kingdom: but the          20
midwives say the children are not in the fault; whereupon the world
increases, and kindreds are mightily strengthened.

POINS  How ill it follows, after you have laboured so hard, you should
    talk so idly! Tell me, how many good young princes would do so,
    their fathers being so sick as yours at this time is.          25

PRINCE  Shall I tell thee one thing, Poins?

POINS  Yes faith, and let it be an excellent good thing.

PRINCE  It shall serve among wits of no higher breeding than thine.

POINS  Go to, I stand the push of your one thing that you will tell.

PRINCE  Marry, I tell thee it is not meet that I should be sad now my          30
    father is sick, albeit I could tell to thee, as to one it pleases me for
    fault of a better to call my friend, I could be sad, and sad indeed too.

POINS  Very hardly, upon such a subject.

PRINCE  By this hand, thou thinkest me as far in the devil's book as thou
    and Falstaff, for obduracy and persistency. Let the end try the          35
    man, but I tell thee my heart bleeds inwardly that my father is so
    sick; and keeping such vile company as thou art hath in reason
    taken from me all ostentation of sorrow.

POINS  The reason?

PRINCE  What wouldst thou think of me if I should weep?          40

POINS  I would think thee a most princely hypocrite.

PRINCE  It would be every man's thought, and thou art a blessed fellow to
    think as every man thinks: never a man's thought in the world keeps
    the roadway better than thine: every man would think me an hypocrite
    indeed; and what accites your most worshipful thought to think so?          45

POINS  Why, because you have been so lewd and so much engraffed to
    Falstaff.

PRINCE  And to thee.

POINS  By this light, I am well spoke on, I can hear it with mine own
    ears: the worst that they can say of me is that I am a second          50
    brother, and that I am a proper fellow of my hands, and those two
    things I confess I cannot help. By the Mass, here comes Bardolph.

*Enter* BARDOLPH *and* [PAGE-] BOY

*Hal comments on the Page's fantastic appearance. Poins and the Page joke about Bardolph's red face. Poins mocks Falstaff's pomposity in continually reminding everyone that he is a knight.*

## 1 Appearance: the Page

Falstaff has dressed his tiny Page in a spectacular uniform. Prince Hal sent the boy as 'Christian' (normally dressed), but Falstaff has 'transformed him ape'.

Design the Page's costume.

## 2 Appearance: Bardolph

Bardolph's drinking has given him a perpetually red face. Poins calls it 'blushing', and the Page is even less flattering. Taverns often had red lattice windows (like a checker board which gave the name 'Chequers' to many pubs). Bardolph's face merges with the red paint!

'Althaea's dream' is the Page's confusion of two stories in Greek mythology. Hecuba dreamed of a firebrand (a burning log), and Althaea was told that her son would live only as long as a firebrand burned.

How important do you think it is for a modern audience to know who Althaea is? How might the Page help the audience to understand the comparison?

## 3 Appearance: fat Falstaff

Poins describes Falstaff as 'the martlemas' (line 78). Martlemas is 11 November, the Feast Day of St Martin. It was traditionally the time of year when cattle and pigs were slaughtered to provide meat for the winter. On the Feast Day there was plenty to eat. Suggest two or three ways in which 'martlemas' is an appropriate label or nickname for Falstaff.

---

**get a pottle-pot's maidenhead** drink the first sip from a half gallon tankard

**e'en now** very recently

**blossom ... cankers!** young boy could be preserved from the corruptions of age!

**wen** wart, swelling

PRINCE And the boy that I gave Falstaff: a had him from me Christian, and look if the fat villain have not transformed him ape.

BARDOLPH God save your grace. 55

PRINCE And yours, most noble Bardolph.

POINS Come, you virtuous ass, you bashful fool, must you be blushing? Wherefore blush you now? What a maidenly man at arms are you become? Is't such a matter to get a pottle-pot's maidenhead?

PAGE A calls me e'en now, my lord, through a red lattice, and I could 60 discern no part of his face from the window; at last I spied his eyes, and methought he had made two holes in the ale-wife's petticoat and so peeped through.

PRINCE Has not the boy profited?

BARDOLPH Away, you whoreson upright rabbit, away! 65

PAGE Away, you rascally Althaea's dream, away!

PRINCE Instruct us, boy: what dream, boy?

PAGE Marry, my lord, Althaea dreamt she was delivered of a firebrand, and therefore I call him her dream.

PRINCE A crown's-worth of good interpretation: there 'tis, boy. 70

POINS O that this blossom could be kept from cankers! Well, there is sixpence to preserve thee.

BARDOLPH And you do not make him hanged among you, the gallows shall have wrong.

PRINCE And how doth thy master, Bardolph? 75

BARDOLPH Well, my lord; he heard of your grace's coming to town: there's a letter for you.

POINS Delivered with good respect. And how doth the martlemas your master?

BARDOLPH In bodily health, sir. 80

POINS Marry, the immortal part needs a physician, but that moves not him: though that be sick, it dies not.

PRINCE I do allow this wen to be as familiar with me as my dog, and he holds his place, for look you how he writes.

*[Hands a letter to Poins]*

POINS *[Reads]* 'John Falstaff, knight' – Every man must know that as 85 oft as he has occasion to name himself: even like those that are kin to the king, for they never prick their finger but they say: 'There's some of the king's blood spilt.' 'How comes that', says he that takes upon him not to conceive. The answer is as ready as a borrower's cap: 'I am the king's poor cousin, sir.' 90

*Falstaff's letter is pompous and self-congratulatory. It warns Hal to beware of Poins. Poins denies the letter's claim. Hal and Poins plan to spy on Falstaff at the Boar's Head Tavern.*

## 1 Falstaff's letter (in pairs)

a Take turns to read the letter aloud in the style that Falstaff probably intends. How might he emphasise in line 97 the echo of Julius Caesar's 'I came, I saw, I conquered'?

b Do you think Falstaff's claim that Poins wants to marry his sister to Hal is true or untrue?

c Suggest several reasons why Falstaff wrote the letter.

d Write out the letter, using a layout and handwriting style that you think is appropriate to Falstaff. If you have a word processor, type out the letter using a typeface and layout that you think Falstaff would choose.

## 2 An aside?

If you were acting Prince Hal, would you speak lines 108–9 ('Well, thus we play ... mock us') as an aside to the audience, to other characters on stage, or to himself? Suggest how each possibility could show a different aspect of Hal's character.

## 3 Sexism? (in small groups)

Imagine someone says to you: 'Hal's two remarks in lines 120 and 128 are sexist.' What would you reply? ('parish heifers' are cows, 'road' is a highway used by everyone.)

---

**fetch it from Japhet** trace their ancestry back to Japhet (in the Bible thought to be the ancestor of all Europeans)
**certificate** formal legal document
**steep** soak
**frank** pigsty

**old place** Boar's Head Tavern
**Ephesians** drinking partners (a joking reference to how they were portrayed in the Bible before they became Christians)
**Pagan** drinking partner

PRINCE   Nay, they will be kin to us, or they will fetch it from Japhet.
But the letter [*Taking it back*]: 'Sir John Falstaff, knight, to the son
of the king nearest his father, Harry Prince of Wales, greeting.'
POINS   Why, this is a certificate.
PRINCE   Peace. 'I will imitate the honourable Romans in brevity–'      95
POINS   He sure means brevity in breath, short-winded.
[PRINCE]   'I commend me to thee, I commend thee, and I leave thee. Be
not too familiar with Poins, for he misuses thy favours so much
that he swears thou art to marry his sister Nell. Repent at idle
times as thou mayst, and so farewell.                                  100
Thine by yea and no, which is as much as to say, as thou usest him:
Jack Falstaff with my familiars; John with my brothers and sisters;
and Sir John with all Europe.'
POINS   My lord, I'll steep this letter in sack and make him eat it.
PRINCE   That's to make him eat twenty of his words. But do you use me   105
thus, Ned? Must I marry your sister?
POINS   God send the wench no worse fortune, but I never said so.
PRINCE   Well, thus we play the fools with the time, and the spirits of the
wise sit in the clouds and mock us. Is your master here in London?
BARDOLPH   Yea, my lord.                                                 110
PRINCE   Where sups he? Doth the old boar feed in the old frank?
BARDOLPH   At the old place, my lord, in Eastcheap.
PRINCE   What company?
PAGE   Ephesians, my lord, of the old church.
PRINCE   Sup any women with him?                                         115
PAGE   None, my lord, but old Mistress Quickly and Mistress Doll
Tearsheet.
PRINCE   What Pagan may that be?
PAGE   A proper gentlewoman, sir, and a kinswoman of my master's.
PRINCE   Even such kin as the parish heifers are to the town bull. Shall  120
we steal upon them, Ned, at supper?
POINS   I am your shadow, my lord, I'll follow you.
PRINCE   Sirrah, you boy and Bardolph, no word to your master that I
am yet come to town; there's for your silence.
BARDOLPH   I have no tongue, sir.                                        125
PAGE   And for mine, sir, I will govern it.
PRINCE   Fare you well: go.

*[Exeunt Page and Bardolph]*

This Doll Tearsheet should be some road.

*Hal and Poins plan to disguise themselves as tavern waiters to spy on Falstaff. In Scene 3, Northumberland begs his wife and daughter-in-law to accept his reasons for joining the rebellion.*

## 1 The ends justify the means

'The purpose must weigh with the folly' says Hal as he looks forward to disguising himself as a 'drawer' or 'prentice' (tavern waiter) to spy on Falstaff. To find how Hal's remark echoes a major theme of the play, turn to page 192.

## 2 'Go not to these wars' (in small groups)

Northumberland, his wife and his daughter-in-law enter in the middle of a conversation. He has decided to join the rebellion, but the two women have protested against that decision. He asks them to understand his 'rough affairs' and not be troublesome to him ('Percy'). His wife is now resigned to his going (lines 5–6) but Lady Percy continues to implore him not to go.

Lady Percy is Kate, the widow of Northumberland's son, Hotspur, who was Prince Hal's opponent in *Part 1*. She embarks on a long speech, reminding Northumberland that, in spite of his promise, he had failed to join Hotspur (who she calls Percy and Harry in line 12) at the battle of Shrewsbury. Her aim is to persuade Northumberland not to join the rebellion.

Share lines 9–45 between you, each person speaking a short section then handing on to the next speaker. Speak as persuasively as possible. You might, for example, emphasise every 'you', to make Northumberland consider all his actions.

After your reading, compile a list of the techniques Lady Percy uses to attempt to persuade her father-in-law.

---

**in his true colours** as he really is
**heavy descension** great fall
**Jove** Greek god who transformed himself into a bull in order to seduce Europa
**weigh with** balance
**even way** sympathetic understanding
**visage** bleak face
**at pawn** promised, at risk
**endeared** committed
**powers** army

POINS  I warrant you, as common as the way between St Albans and
    London.                                                                                              130
PRINCE  How might we see Falstaff bestow himself tonight in his true
    colours, and not ourselves be seen?
POINS  Put on two leathern jerkins and aprons, and wait upon him at
    his table as drawers.
PRINCE  From a god to a bull: a heavy descension! It was Jove's case.      135
    From a prince to a prentice: a low transformation, that shall be
    mine; for in everything the purpose must weigh with the folly.
    Follow me, Ned.

*Exeunt*


# ACT 2    SCENE 3
## Warkworth Castle


*Enter* NORTHUMBERLAND, *his* LADY, *and* LADY PERCY,
*wife to Harry Percy*

NORTHUMBERLAND  I pray thee, loving wife, and gentle daughter,
    Give even way unto my rough affairs:
    Put not you on the visage of the times
    And be like them to Percy troublesome.
LADY NORTHUMBERLAND  I have given over, I will speak no more,        5
    Do what you will, your wisdom be your guide.
NORTHUMBERLAND  Alas, sweet wife, my honour is at pawn,
    And, but my going, nothing can redeem it.
LADY PERCY  O, yet for God's sake go not to these wars;
    The time was, father, that you broke your word,                    10
    When you were more endeared to it than now,
    When your own Percy, when my heart's dear Harry
    Threw many a northward look to see his father
    Bring up his powers, but he did long in vain.
    Who then persuaded you to stay at home?                             15

*Lady Percy recalls that Hotspur's brilliant qualities were copied by every nobleman. But Northumberland failed to join him in battle. Northumberland's wife urges him to wait to see how the rebels succeed.*

Lady Percy (left) portrays her dead husband Hotspur as an outstanding figure of chivalry as she tries to persuade Northumberland not to fight.

## 1 'Speaking thick' (in groups of three)

Lady Percy claims that all the noblemen ('chivalry') of England took Hotspur as their model or mirror ('glass'). They copied his walk ('gait'), his dress and his voice. For the Elizabethans, 'speaking thick' probably meant fast and loud. But some actors have interpreted it as speaking with a strong Northern accent.

The three characters in this short scene are Hotspur's closest relatives. How do they speak? Talk together about what accents they might use. The true test is to take parts and speak the scene.

| | |
|---|---|
| **grey vault** azure sky | **defensible** powerful |
| **Became** adorned, were adopted as | **precise and nice** punctiliously, |
| **tardily** slowly | carefully measured |
| **humours of blood** moods | **Monmouth's** Prince Hal's |
| **mark** model | **Beshrew** curse (a mild oath) |
| **unseconded** unsupported | **ancient oversights** old mistakes |
| **abide a field** fight a battle | **puissance** powers, army |

There were two honours lost: yours and your son's.
For yours, the God of heaven brighten it;
For his, it stuck upon him as the sun
In the grey vault of heaven, and by his light
Did all the chivalry of England move                              20
To do brave acts. He was indeed the glass
Wherein the noble youth did dress themselves.
He had no legs that practised not his gait;
And speaking thick, which Nature made his blemish,
Became the accents of the valiant,                                25
For those that could speak low and tardily
Would turn their own perfection to abuse
To seem like him. So that in speech, in gait,
In diet, in affections of delight,
In military rules, humours of blood,                              30
He was the mark and glass, copy and book,
That fashioned others. And him – O wondrous! – him –
O miracle of men! – him did you leave,
Second to none, unseconded by you,
To look upon the hideous god of war                               35
In disadvantage, to abide a field
Where nothing but the sound of Hotspur's name
Did seem defensible: so you left him.
Never, O never do his ghost the wrong
To hold your honour more precise and nice                         40
With others than with him. Let them alone:
The marshal and the archbishop are strong.
Had my sweet Harry had but half their numbers,
Today might I, hanging on Hotspur's neck,
Have talked of Monmouth's grave.

NORTHUMBERLAND                          Beshrew your heart,        45
Fair daughter, you do draw my spirits from me
With new lamenting ancient oversights.
But I must go and meet with danger there,
Or it will seek me in another place
And find me worse provided.

LADY NORTHUMBERLAND                     O fly to Scotland,         50
Till that the nobles and the armèd commons
Have of their puissance made a little taste.

*Lady Percy urges Northumberland to delay until the outcome of the rebels' battle against the king. He decides to wait. In Scene 4, the tavern waiters prepare for the entry of Falstaff, Hal and Poins.*

## 1 Final appearances (in small groups)

Lady Northumberland and Lady Percy appear only in this scene, and Northumberland never appears again. Consider each character in turn, giving your impression of him or her. For example, is Northumberland really persuaded by the women's arguments, or had he secretly decided from the start not to join the rebels?

## 2 The tavern scene (whole class)

Use the following sections of Scene 4 to help you plan how you work on the scene. For example, different groups might take responsibility to prepare and enact different episodes.

lines 1–16   The waiters prepare the room.

lines 17–87   The Hostess, Doll and Falstaff.

lines 88–167   Ancient Pistol.

lines 168–285   Prince Hal, Poins, Falstaff and Doll.

lines 286–320   News of the war.

## 3 Costume change?

Shakespeare may have inserted lines 1–16 to give time for a costume change. In his day, women's parts were played by boys, so the two boys who played Lady Northumberland and Lady Percy in the previous scene may have doubled as the Hostess and Doll Tearsheet in Scene 4. The waiters' sixteen lines, together with appropriate 'business' (stage action), could provide time for the costume change.

---

**get ground and vantage of** win the first battle against
**try** fight the first battle
**rain upon remembrance** drop tears on rosemary (herb of remembrance)
**still stand** stand still, pause

**time and vantage** opportunity
**crave** invite, long for
**apple-johns** old withered apples
**Mass** by the Mass (a mild oath)
**cover** spread the tablecloth
**Sneak's noise** Sneak's band
**fain** gladly

LADY PERCY  If they get ground and vantage of the king,
    Then join you with them like a rib of steel
    To make strength stronger; but, for all our loves,    55
    First let them try themselves: so did your son,
    He was so suffered, so came I a widow,
    And never shall have length of life enough
    To rain upon remembrance with mine eyes,
    That it may grow and sprout as high as heaven    60
    For recordation to my noble husband.
NORTHUMBERLAND  Come, come, go in with me: 'tis with my mind
    As with the tide swelled up unto his height
    That makes a still stand, running neither way.
    Fain would I go to meet the archbishop,    65
    But many thousand reasons hold me back.
    I will resolve for Scotland: there am I
    Till time and vantage crave my company.

*Exeunt*


# ACT 2   SCENE 4
## London: the Boar's Head Tavern


*Enter* FRANCIS *and another* DRAWER

FRANCIS  What the devil hast thou brought there: apple-johns? Thou
knowest Sir John cannot endure an apple-john.
DRAWER  Mass, thou sayst true: the prince once set a dish of apple-johns
before him and told him there were five more Sir Johns, and putting
off his hat said 'I will now take my leave of these six dry, round, old,   5
withered knights.' It angered him to the heart, but he hath forgot that.
FRANCIS  Why then, cover and set them down, and see if thou canst
find out Sneak's noise: Mistress Tearsheet would fain hear some
music. Dispatch: the room where they supped is too hot, they'll
come in straight.   10

*Enter* WILL

WILL  Sirrah, here will be the prince and Master Poins anon, and they
will put on two of our jerkins and aprons, and Sir John must not
know of it: Bardolph hath brought word.

*Doll Tearsheet has drunk too much wine, but the Hostess compliments her on her appearance. Falstaff accuses Doll of spreading sexual diseases. Their language is full of sexual innuendo.*

## 1 Mangling the language

Hostess Quickly's language is a riot of misused words. When she says that Doll is 'sick of a calm', she probably means 'qualm' or stomach upset. Make a guess at what you think she intends when she says 'temperality', 'pulsidge' and 'perfumes' (lines 18–21).

## 2 'Empty the jordan'

In both Henry IV's time and in Shakespeare's, sanitation was extremely basic. 'Jordans' (chamberpots) were in common use, and few people were embarrassed by them. Imagine you are directing the play. Suggest how you would stage Falstaff's line 27 and the servant's exit.

## 3 Sexual language (in groups of three)

Much of what Doll and Falstaff say to each other is charged with sexual meaning. Take parts and speak lines 26–44, then talk together about your views on how the sexual language might be delivered on stage. Use the following explanations to help you:

'pox' (line 32) – sexually transmitted diseases, syphilis

'fat rascals' (line 34) – bloated young deer (syphilis was thought to make the sufferer fat)

'brooches, pearls and ouches' (line 40) – scabs of sexually transmitted diseases

'serve bravely ... chambers' (lines 40–3) – a series of military metaphors, all with sexual meanings

old utis  high jinks, great fun
canaries  wine from the Canary
 Islands
hem  hiccough
When Arthur first in court
 (from a popular ballad)

sect  sex, profession as a prostitute
breach  hole in defences
conger  eel, penis

FRANCIS  By the Mass, here will be old utis: it will be an excellent
    stratagem.                                                                   15
DRAWER  I'll see if I can find out Sneak.

*Exit [with Francis]*

*Enter* HOSTESS *and* DOLL TEARSHEET

HOSTESS  I'faith, sweetheart, methinks now you are in an excellent
    good temperality. Your pulsidge beats as extraordinarily as heart
    would desire, and your colour, I warrant you, is as red as any rose,
    in good truth, la; but i'faith, you have drunk too much canaries,    20
    and that's a marvellous searching wine, and it perfumes the blood
    ere one can say 'What's this.' How do you now?
DOLL  Better than I was – hem.
HOSTESS  Why, that's well said: a good heart's worth gold. – Lo, here
    comes Sir John.                                                              25

*Enter* FALSTAFF [, *singing*]

FALSTAFF  When Arthur first in court –
    Empty the jordan –

*[Exit Will]*

    And was a worthy king –
    How now, Mistress Doll?
HOSTESS  Sick of a calm, yea, good faith.                                        30
FALSTAFF  So is all her sect: and they be once in a calm they are sick.
DOLL  A pox damn you, you muddy rascal, is that all the comfort you
    give me?
FALSTAFF  You make fat rascals, Mistress Doll.
DOLL  I make them? Gluttony and diseases make them, I make them not.   35
FALSTAFF  If the cook help to make the gluttony, you help to make the
    diseases, Doll; we catch of you, Doll, we catch of you. Grant that,
    my poor virtue, grant that.
DOLL  Yea, joy, our chains and our jewels.
FALSTAFF  Your brooches, pearls and ouches – for to serve bravely is to  40
    come halting off, you know; to come off the breach with his pike
    bent bravely; and to surgery bravely; to venture upon the charged
    chambers bravely –
DOLL  Hang yourself, you muddy conger, hang yourself.

*The Hostess succeeds in persuading Doll to become friends with Falstaff.*
*Doll is enraged to hear of Pistol, and the Hostess refuses to admit him*
*because he will lower her tavern's reputation.*

## 1 Speak as Hostess Quickly (in pairs)

The Hostess continues to spray her language with inventive imagination.
She says that Doll and Falstaff grate on each other like 'two dry toasts'.
Perhaps when she calls them 'rheumatic' she means 'choleric' or angry
(choler was believed to be one of the four humours which governed
human temperament). By 'confirmities' she probably means infirmities.

Hearing of Pistol, she explodes against 'swaggerers': boastful and
blustering soldiers whose loud, unpredictable behaviour would bring
her tavern into disrepute. She tells of a warning she has received from
the magistrate, advising her to keep such characters as Pistol out of her
tavern.

Take turns to speak all the Hostess' language up to line 87 to help
you deepen your impression of her personality.

## 2 First news of Ancient Pistol (in pairs)

Pistol has made a great impression on the Hostess as a swaggerer. He
will shortly make his entrance. Falstaff wants Pistol to come in,
describing him as his ancient (ensign or standard bearer) and as a 'tame
cheater' (harmless con man).

Tell you partner of your expectation of what Pistol will be like from
what is said opposite. When he enters, see if he matches your expectation.

---

**What the good-year!** good
 heavens!
**bear** endure
**hogshead** large barrel
**merchant's venture** cargo
**Bordeaux stuff** French wine
**hulk** large ship

**name and fame** reputation
**Tilly-vally** nonsense!
**debuty** magistrate (deputy)
**in an ill name** keep a disorderly
 tavern
**Barbary hen** prostitute

HOSTESS  By my troth, this is the old fashion: you two never meet but   45
you fall to some discord; you are both, i'good truth, as rheumatic
as two dry toasts, you cannot one bear with another's confirmities.
What the good-year! One must bear, and that must be you, you
are the weaker vessel, as they say, the emptier vessel.

DOLL   Can a weak empty vessel bear such a huge full hogshead?   50
There's a whole merchant's venture of Bordeaux stuff in him: you
have not seen a hulk better stuffed in the hold. Come, I'll be
friends with thee, Jack: thou art going to the wars, and whether I
shall ever see thee again or no, there is nobody cares.

*Enter* DRAWER

DRAWER  Sir, Ancient Pistol's below, and would speak with you.   55
DOLL  Hang him, swaggering rascal, let him not come hither. It is the
foul-mouthedst rogue in England.
HOSTESS  If he swagger, let him not come here. No, by my faith, I must
live among my neighbours, I'll no swaggerers, I am in good name
and fame with the very best. Shut the door, there comes no   60
swaggerers here: I have not lived all this while to have swaggering
now. Shut the door I pray you.
FALSTAFF  Dost thou hear, hostess?
HOSTESS  Pray ye pacify yourself, Sir John, there comes no swaggerers
here.   65
FALSTAFF  Dost thou hear? It is mine ancient.
HOSTESS  Tilly-vally, Sir John, ne'er tell me. And your ancient swagger, a
comes not in my doors. I was before Master Tisick the debuty t'other
day, and as he said to me – 'twas no longer ago than Wedsday last, ay,
good faith – 'Neighbour Quickly', says he – Master Dumb our   70
minister was by then – 'Neighbour Quickly', says he, 'receive those
that are civil, for', said he, 'you are in an ill name.' Now a said so, I can
tell whereupon. 'For', says he, 'you are an honest woman, and well
thought on, therefore take heed what guests you receive; receive',
says he, 'no swaggering companions.' There comes none here. You   75
would bless you to hear what he said! No, I'll no swaggerers.
FALSTAFF  He's no swaggerer, hostess, a tame cheater, i'faith, you may
stroke him as gently as a puppy greyhound; he'll not swagger with
a Barbary hen if her feathers turn back in any show of resistance.
Call him up, drawer.   80

*The Hostess continues to complain how she detests rowdy customers. Pistol's entry produces a stream of sexually charged language from everyone. Doll vehemently reviles Pistol.*

Ancient Pistol. Doll calls him 'lack-linen' (shirt-less), a pickpocket ('cutpurse', 'filthy bung'), and accuses him of being a pimp, someone who lives off prostitutes' earnings ('stewed prunes and dried cakes' were provided in brothels because they were believed to protect against sexually transmitted disease).

## 1 Torrents of language

Using sexually ambiguous language, Falstaff invites Pistol to drink a toast to the Hostess. Pistol's reply is full of sexual innuendo. Doll unleashes a torrent of abuse, jeering at Pistol's claim to be a soldier, outraged to hear him called 'Captain'. Speak all Doll's lines opposite, putting as much venom into her insults as possible.

| | |
|---|---|
| **bar** deny entry to | **Since when** since when have you been a soldier? |
| **charge** drink a toast to | |
| **bullets** (testicles) | **points** laces to tie armour |
| **mouldy chaps** poxy cheeks | **ruff** collar |
| **cuttle** pickpocket's knife | **'occupy'** 'fornicate' |
| **basket-hilt** old-fashioned sword hilt | **was ill-sorted** kept bad companions |

HOSTESS  Cheater call you him? I will bar no honest man my house, nor no cheater, but I do not love swaggering; by my troth, I am the worse when one says 'swagger'. Feel, masters, how I shake, look you, I warrant you.

DOLL  So you do, hostess.                                                                                                 85

HOSTESS  Do I? Yea in very truth do I, and 'twere an aspen leaf. I cannot abide swaggerers.

*Enter Ancient* PISTOL, BARDOLPH *and* PAGE

PISTOL  God save you, Sir John.

FALSTAFF  Welcome, Ancient Pistol. Here, Pistol, I charge you with a cup of sack: do you discharge upon mine hostess.                         90

PISTOL  I will discharge upon her, Sir John, with two bullets.

FALSTAFF  She is pistol-proof, sir: you shall not hardly offend her.

HOSTESS  Come, I'll drink no proofs, nor no bullets; I'll drink no more than will do me good for no man's pleasure, I.

PISTOL  Then to you, Mistress Dorothy: I will charge you.                          95

DOLL  Charge me? I scorn you, scurvy companion. What, you poor, base, rascally, cheating, lack-linen mate! Away, you mouldy rogue, away, I am meat for your master.

PISTOL  I know you, Mistress Dorothy.

DOLL  Away, you cutpurse rascal, you filthy bung, away. By this wine,          100
I'll thrust my knife in your mouldy chaps, and you play the saucy cuttle with me. Away, you bottle-ale rascal, you basket-hilt stale juggler, you. Since when, I pray you, sir? God's light, with two points on your shoulder? Much!

PISTOL  God let me not live, but I will murther your ruff for this.          105

FALSTAFF  No more, Pistol, I would not have you go off here: discharge yourself of our company, Pistol.

HOSTESS  No, good Captain Pistol, not here, sweet captain.

DOLL  Captain? Thou abominable damned cheater, art thou not ashamed to be called captain? And captains were of my mind, they          110
would truncheon you out for taking their names upon you before you have earned them. You a captain? You slave, for what? For tearing a poor whore's ruff in a bawdy-house? He a captain? Hang him, rogue, he lives upon mouldy stewed prunes and dried cakes. A captain? God's light, these villains will make the word as odious          115
as the word 'occupy', which was an excellent good word before it was ill-sorted, therefore captains had need look to't.

*Pistol rants wildly, quoting half-remembered lines of old plays and mock-Italian. The Hostess tries to calm him, but Doll and Falstaff order him to be kicked downstairs.*

## 1 Pistol fires off (in groups of six)

Ancient Pistol (who may be very drunk) uses bombast: a high-flown, declamatory style of language. He often mis-quotes from Elizabethan plays that revelled in spectacle and over-the-top language.

Share out the parts, and take turns to speak as Pistol in lines 88–167. Don't worry about the meaning of his words; Pistol himself probably doesn't understand much of what he is saying – but he likes the sound of it! The following may help you make some sense of what he says.

lines 123–5 'Pluto's damnèd lake' is the god of Hell's river Styx; Erebus is Hell (the son of Chaos and brother of Night).

lines 127, 140 'Hiren' is probably the name of Pistol's sword, perhaps after Irene (peace) from an old play.

lines 130–2 A part-remembered quotation from a very popular Elizabethan play, *Tamburlaine* by Christopher Marlowe. Tamburlaine has replaced the horses that draw his chariot with kings he has captured. He flogs the exhausted kings and cries: 'Holla, you pampered jades of Asia,/What, can ye draw but twenty miles a day?'

line 135 'Cerberus' is the three-headed watch-dog of Hell.

line 139 'give crowns like pins!' is another echo of Tamburlaine who made his captains kings.

line 143 Calipolis was a character in a play who is offered lion meat on a sword.

line 145 'If fortune torments me, hope contents me.'

line 153 Galloway nags are prostitutes.

---

**faitors** traitors
**aggravate** abate (the Hostess' malapropism)
**welkin** sky
**fall foul for toys** fall out over trifles
**broadsides** volleys of gunfire

**full points** sword points
**etceteras/things** female sex organs
**neaf** hand
**fustian** ranting, old fashioned
**Quoit** shove
**shove-groat shilling** coin used in shove-halfpenny

BARDOLPH  Pray thee go down, good ancient.

FALSTAFF  Hark thee hither, Mistress Doll.

PISTOL  Not I. I tell thee what, Corporal Bardolph: I could tear her, I'll    120
be revenged of her.

PAGE  Pray thee go down.

PISTOL  I'll see her damned first. To Pluto's damnèd lake – by this hand!
To th'infernal deep,
            With Erebus and tortures vile also.    125
Hold hook and line, say I, down, down, dogs, down faitors:
            Have we not Hiren here?

HOSTESS  Good Captain Peesel, be quiet, 'tis very late, i'faith. I beseek
you now, aggravate your choler.

PISTOL  These be good humours indeed! Shall pack-horses    130
            And hollow pampered jades of Asia,
            Which cannot go but thirty mile a day,
            Compare with Caesars, and with Cannibals,
            And Troyant Greeks?
            Nay, rather damn them with King Cerberus,    135
            And let the welkin roar. – Shall we fall foul for toys?

HOSTESS  By my troth, captain, these are very bitter words.

BARDOLPH  Be gone, good ancient; this will grow to a brawl anon.

PISTOL  Die men like dogs, give crowns like pins!
            Have we not Hiren here?    140

HOSTESS  A'my word, captain, there's none such here. What the
goodyear, do you think I would deny her? For God's sake, be quiet.

PISTOL  Then feed and be fat, my fair Calipolis –
Come, give's some sack.
[Sings] Se fortuna mi tormenta, ben sperato mi contenta –    145
            Fear we broadsides? No, let the fiend give fire –
Give me some sack! [To his sword] And sweetheart, lie thou there.
Come we to full points here? and are etceteras no things?

FALSTAFF  Pistol, I would be quiet.

PISTOL  Sweet knight, I kiss thy neaf. What, we have seen the seven stars.    150

DOLL  For God's sake, thrust him downstairs, I cannot endure such a
fustian rascal.

PISTOL  Thrust him downstairs? Know we not Galloway nags?

FALSTAFF  Quoit him down, Bardolph, like a shove-groat shilling. Nay,
and a do nothing but speak nothing, a shall be nothing here.    155

> *Pistol continues to rant, but is driven out of the room. Doll praises Falstaff's bravery. The musicians play. Falstaff boasts of his fighting skill, but Doll begs him to reform his ways.*

## 1 Driving out Pistol (in small groups)

Pistol erupted into the tavern with an explosion of words, but is finally driven out. But by whom? Bardolph reports that Falstaff wounded Pistol, and Falstaff brags about how quickly Pistol ran from him. But why does Doll say that Falstaff followed 'him like a church'? Churches don't move!

Work out how to stage Pistol's exit, showing what part Falstaff plays. If you decide that there actually was a fight, follow the first rule of all stage combat: safety. Make sure nobody gets hurt, however spectacular the fighting might appear to the audience.

## 2 A change of mood

After the tumult caused by Pistol, a quieter mood settles on the Boar's Head. Doll comforts Falstaff and speaks tenderly to him. She praises his bravery, comparing him with heroes in Greek legend. At the siege of Troy, Hector was the Trojans' best warrior, and Agamemnon led the Greek army. The nine Worthies were nine famous heroes (who often appeared in folk plays and romances).

How sincere is Doll in what she says to Falstaff?

## 3 The musicians

The musicians who arrive and play are 'Sneak's noise' (see line 8). As you read on, think about the kind of music they are likely to play.

---

**incision** blood-letting
**imbrue** cover in blood
**sisters three** three Fates who spun the thread of life (in Greek myth)
**Atropos** a Fate who cut the thread of life
**tirrits** terrible fits

**brave** challenge, defy
**chops** fat cheeks
**canvas** meet
**Bartholomew boar-pig** roast pigs were served at Bartholomew Fair, held on 24 August each year
**foining** fornicating

BARDOLPH Come, get you downstairs.

PISTOL   What, shall we have incision? Shall we imbrue?
    Then Death rock me asleep, abridge my doleful days!
    Why then, let grievous ghastly gaping wounds
    Untwind the sisters three; come, Atropos, I say!   160

HOSTESS Here's goodly stuff toward.

FALSTAFF Give me my rapier, boy.

DOLL I pray thee, Jack, I pray thee, do not draw.

FALSTAFF Get you downstairs.

HOSTESS Here's a goodly tumult: I'll forswear keeping house afore I'll   165
    be in these tirrits and frights. So: murder I warrant, now. Alas,
    alas, put up your naked weapons, put up your naked weapons.

                    [*Exeunt Pistol and Bardolph*]

DOLL I pray thee, Jack, be quiet, the rascal's gone. Ah, you whoreson
    little valiant villain, you!

HOSTESS Are you not hurt i'th'groin? Methought a made a shrewd   170
    thrust at your belly.

                    [*Enter* BARDOLPH]

FALSTAFF Have you turned him out a'doors?

BARDOLPH   Yea, sir; the rascal's drunk, you have hurt him, sir,
    i'th'shoulder.

FALSTAFF A rascal to brave me!   175

DOLL   Ah, you sweet little rogue, you! Alas, poor ape, how thou
    sweatest! Come, let me wipe thy face: come on, you whoreson
    chops. Ah, rogue, i'faith I love thee. Thou art as valorous as
    Hector of Troy, worth five of Agamemnon, and ten times better
    than the nine Worthies. Ah, villain!   180

FALSTAFF Ah, rascally slave! I will toss the rogue in a blanket.

DOLL Do, and thou darest for thy heart; and thou dost, I'll canvas thee
    between a pair of sheets.

PAGE The music is come, sir.

                    *Enter* MUSIC

FALSTAFF Let them play. – Play, sirs. Sit on my knee, Doll. A rascal   185
    bragging slave! The rogue fled from me like quicksilver.

DOLL I'faith, and thou followedst him like a church. Thou whoreson little
    tidy Bartholomew boar-pig, when wilt thou leave fighting a–days
    and foining a–nights, and begin to patch up thine old body for heaven?

*Poins and Hal, disguised as waiters, hear Falstaff insultingly describe their characters. They comment in similar fashion on his behaviour. Falstaff wants Doll to comfort him.*

## 1 Is Doll in the secret? (in small groups)

Hal and Poins are dressed as tavern waiters. They overhear Falstaff respond to Doll's questions about them. How do they hide, and is Doll an accomplice to the joke? Work out the dramatic effect of, first, that she knows Hal and Poins are listening; second, that she doesn't.

## 2 Describing Poins

Falstaff's description of Poins gives an insight into Shakespeare's England. Most of Poins 'gambol faculties' (playful habits) refer to lively games or fashions of the times. Match each of the following with Falstaff's lines 200–8:

- Men's costumes showed off the shape of their legs.
- 'quoits' a game like pitching horseshoes.
- 'conger' eating eels was thought to breed stupidity.
- 'candles' ends for flap-dragons' a pub game in which competitors drank from tankards containing lighted candles.
- 'the wild mare' a very boisterous version of leapfrog or seesaw.
- 'joint-stools' another pub game of leaping over wooden stools.
- 'breeds no bate … stories' causes no quarrels by his gossiping.

## 3 Astrological comparisons

Hal and Poins use astrology to describe Falstaff, Doll and Bardolph. 'Saturn and Venus' represented old age and love; an 'almanac' was an astrologer's chart on which the twelve signs of the Zodiac were divided into four triangles (trigons). One trigon contained the three most fiery ones: Aries, Leo and Sagittarius.

---

**death's-head** reminder of death
**pantler** servant who sliced bread
**conceit** wittiness, wit
**sign of the Leg** shoe-shop sign
**avoirdupois** weight
**nave of a wheel** round knave

**ears cut off** punishment for
  slander
**poll** head
**lisping to … counsel-keeper!**
  flirting with the Hostess
**busses** kisses
**kirtle** dress

*Enter the* PRINCE *and* POINS *disguised*

FALSTAFF  Peace, good Doll, do not speak like a death's-head, do not    190
bid me remember mine end.

DOLL  Sirrah, what humour's the prince of?

FALSTAFF  A good shallow young fellow, a would have made a good
pantler, a would ha'chipped bread well.

DOLL  They say Poins has a good wit.    195

FALSTAFF  He a good wit? Hang him, baboon: his wit's as thick as
Tewkesbury mustard, there's no more conceit in him than is in a
mallet.

DOLL  Why does the prince love him so, then?

FALSTAFF  Because their legs are both of a bigness, and a plays at quoits    200
well, and eats conger and fennel, and drinks off candles' ends for
flap-dragons, and rides the wild mare with the boys, and jumps
upon joint-stools, and swears with a good grace, and wears his
boots very smooth like unto the sign of the Leg, and breeds no
bate with telling of discreet stories, and such other gambol faculties    205
a has that show a weak mind and an able body, for the which the
prince admits him; for the prince himself is such another: the
weight of a hair will turn scales between their avoirdupois.

PRINCE  Would not this nave of a wheel have his ears cut off?

POINS  Let's beat him before his whore.    210

PRINCE  Look whe'er the withered elder hath not his poll clawed like
a parrot.

POINS  Is it not strange that desire should so many years outlive
performance?

FALSTAFF  Kiss me, Doll.    215

PRINCE  Saturn and Venus this year in conjunction? What says
th'almanac to that?

POINS  And look whether the fiery trigon his man be not lisping to his
master's old tables, his notebook, his counsel-keeper!

FALSTAFF  Thou dost give me flattering busses.    220

DOLL  By my troth, I kiss thee with a most constant heart.

FALSTAFF  I am old, I am old.

DOLL  I love thee better than I love e'er a scurvy young boy of them all.

FALSTAFF  What stuff wilt have a kirtle of? I shall receive money a-
Thursday – shalt have a cap tomorrow. A merry song, come;    225
a-grows late, we'll to bed. Thou'lt forget me when I am gone.

*Hal and Poins throw off their disguise. Falstaff denies that he knew they were listening to him. He claims he insulted Hal to prevent wicked people falling in love with the prince.*

## 1 Echoes of *Part 1* (in small groups)

Stage the episode (lines 229–63) in which Hal and Poins accuse Falstaff, who tries to talk his way out of his predicament. The following two reminders of events in *Part 1* can help you:

- (line 230) Hal and Poins played a joke on Francis, the tavern waiter. As Hal talked to Francis, Poins kept calling him. Francis became thoroughly confused, repeating 'Anon, anon, sir' as he tried to attend to each of his tormentors.
- (lines 248–9) Falstaff robbed some travellers at Gad's Hill, and was in turn robbed by Hal and Poins who were disguised. Later, Falstaff falsely claimed that he knew all along that his assailants were Hal and Poins.

Now Falstaff denies he knew that Hal was listening and offers a different reason to excuse his mocking of the prince and Poins. He uses the language of Puritan preachers in denouncing 'the wicked', saying that his disparagement of Hal was to ensure that 'the wicked may not fall in love with thee'.

When you turn the page you will find how Hal picks up the phrase 'the wicked' and uses it against Falstaff.

## 2 Recognition?

Just when does Falstaff recognise Hal and Poins? Step into Falstaff's shoes and say whether you first recognise them at line 231, or line 234, or line 239.

---

**prove that**  forbid that
**of sinful continents**  filled with
  large sinful parts
**take not the heat**  don't act
  immediately

**candle-mine**  pit of fat (from
  which candles could be mined)
**vildly**  vilely, insultingly

DOLL  By my troth, thou'lt set me a-weeping and thou sayst so; prove that
    ever I dress myself handsome till thy return! Well, hearken a'th'end.
FALSTAFF  Some sack, Francis!
PRINCE *and* POINS  Anon, anon, sir.                                      230
FALSTAFF  Ha? A bastard son of the king's? And art not thou Poins his
    brother?
PRINCE  Why, thou globe of sinful continents, what a life dost thou lead?
FALSTAFF  A better than thou: I am a gentleman, thou art a drawer.
PRINCE  Very true, sir; and I come to draw you out by the ears.           235
HOSTESS  O, the Lord preserve thy grace! By my troth, welcome to
    London. Now the Lord bless that sweet face of thine. O Jesu, are
    you come from Wales?
FALSTAFF  Thou whoreson mad compound of majesty, by this light –
    flesh and corrupt blood [*Placing his hand on Doll*], thou art welcome.  240
DOLL  How? You fat fool, I scorn you.
POINS  My lord, he will drive you out of your revenge, and turn all to
    a merriment, if you take not the heat.
PRINCE  You whoreson candle-mine, you, how vildly did you speak of
    me now, before this honest, virtuous, civil gentlewoman?             245
HOSTESS  God's blessing of your good heart, and so she is, by my troth.
FALSTAFF  Didst thou hear me?
PRINCE  Yea, and you knew me as you did when you ran away by Gad's
    Hill – you knew I was at your back, and spoke it on purpose to try
    my patience.                                                         250
FALSTAFF  No, no, no, not so: I did not think thou wast within hearing.
PRINCE  I shall drive you then to confess the wilful abuse, and then I
    know how to handle you.
FALSTAFF  No abuse, Hal, a'mine honour, no abuse.
PRINCE  Not – to dispraise me, and call me pantler and bread-chipper     255
    and I know not what?
FALSTAFF  No abuse, Hal.
POINS  No abuse?
FALSTAFF  No abuse, Ned, i'th'world, honest Ned, none. I dispraised
    him before the wicked, that the wicked might not fall in love with   260
    thee; in which doing I have done the part of a careful friend and
    a true subject, and thy father is to give me thanks for it. No abuse,
    Hal, none, Ned, none; no, faith, boys, none.

*Hal asks Falstaff if all his tavern companions are wicked. Falstaff says only the Hostess might be excused the charge. Peto brings news of preparations for war.*

## 1 'The wicked'

Falstaff had imitated the language of the Puritan preachers of Shakespeare's time, who proclaimed that 'the wicked' (anyone who was not a Puritan) were damned and would burn in Hell. Hal demands to know just who Falstaff thinks is wicked.

Falstaff claims that Bardolph, his Page and Doll are damned, but the Hostess might not be, although she has loaned money (considered by many to be a sin). Falstaff levels a different charge against the Hostess: that she allowed meat to be eaten in the tavern. There were Elizabethan laws that decreed certain meat-free days, in order to encourage the eating of fish. In the Christian Church, Lent (the period before Easter) was also supposed to be a time of abstinence from meat-eating.

But both Falstaff and the Hostess may not be thinking about meat-eating, but about prostitution. Both 'flesh' and 'mutton' were nicknames for prostitutes.

Use the information above to suggest what Hal was going to say to Doll at line 283 (perhaps Falstaff's line 285 is a clue).

## 2 A change of mood (in pairs)

Peto's loud knocking, and his news of war, signal another change of mood in the scene. If you were directing the play, what reaction from the audience would you wish to evoke at lines 286–93? Describe how you would try to achieve that response (lighting, sound, movement, facial expressions, actors' tone of voice, and so on).

---

**close** make peace
**zeal** faith, essence
**The fiend** the devil
**pricked down** recruited
 (see page 104)
**Lucifer's privy kitchen**
 the devil's private kitchen

**malt-worms** drunkards
**burns** infects
**indictment** accusation, charge
**vict'lers** victuallers, innkeepers
**posts** messengers on horses
**Bare-headed** in great haste

76

PRINCE  See now whether pure fear and entire cowardice doth not make thee wrong this virtuous gentlewoman, to close with us! Is she of the wicked, is thine hostess here of the wicked, or is thy boy of the wicked, or honest Bardolph, whose zeal burns in his nose, of the wicked? 265

POINS  Answer, thou dead elm, answer.

FALSTAFF  The fiend hath pricked down Bardolph irrecoverable, and his face is Lucifer's privy kitchen, where he doth nothing but roast malt-worms. For the boy, there is a good angel about him, but the devil blinds him too. 270

PRINCE  For the women?

FALSTAFF  For one of them, she's in hell already, and burns poor souls; for th'other, I owe her money, and whether she be damned for that I know not. 275

HOSTESS  No, I warrant you.

FALSTAFF  No, I think thou art not, I think thou art quit for that. Marry, there is another indictment upon thee, for suffering flesh to be eaten in thy house, contrary to the law, for the which I think thou wilt howl. 280

HOSTESS  All vict'lers do so; what's a joint of mutton or two in a whole Lent?

PRINCE  You, gentlewoman –

DOLL  What says your grace?

FALSTAFF  His grace says that which his flesh rebels against. 285

PETO k*nocks at door*

HOSTESS  Who knocks so loud at door? Look to th'door there, Francis.

*Enter* PETO

PRINCE  Peto, how now, what news?

PETO  The king your father is at Westminster,
And there are twenty weak and wearied posts
Come from the North, and as I came along 290
I met and overtook a dozen captains
Bare-headed, sweating, knocking at the taverns,
And asking everyone for Sir John Falstaff.

*Hal feels shame at wasting his time frivolously whilst war threatens. He leaves. Falstaff regrets he cannot stay the night, and, boasting, also leaves. Bardolph returns to tell Doll to go to Falstaff.*

## 1 Departures for the war (in small groups)

The scene closes in a bustle of action. In one production, sounds of preparation for the coming war were heard. Loud military music played, and the noise of marching and sharpening of weapons accompanied the various speeches and departures.

Work out how you would end the scene (from line 294) to greatest dramatic effect. Prepare notes for each actor about how their lines should be spoken and how each exit could be staged. Don't forget the musicians. Then allocate parts and act out your scene ending.

## 2 Has she learned from experience?

Think about what lines 313–15 suggest about the relationship of the Hostess and Falstaff. What emotions do you feel when the Hostess describes Falstaff as 'an honester and truer-hearted man'?

## 3 Looking back: point of view

Choose one character who has appeared in Scene 4. As that character, tell the story of what you saw, heard and felt throughout the scene.

## 4 Falstaff: brave or cowardly?

Why do a dozen captains await Falstaff outside the tavern? Do they see him as a great leader? In three or four sentences, give your own impression of Falstaff at this point in the play.

---

**profane** desecrate, dishonour
**commotion** rebellion
**south** south wind
**post** hastily

**peascod time** early summer when peas ripen
**blubbered** tear-stained

PRINCE  By heaven, Poins, I feel me much to blame
So idly to profane the precious time,                                    295
When tempest of commotion, like the south,
Borne with black vapour, doth begin to melt
And drop upon our bare unarmèd heads.
Give me my sword and cloak. Falstaff, good night.

*Exeunt Prince, Poins [, Bardolph and Peto]*

FALSTAFF  Now comes in the sweetest morsel of the night, and we must    300
hence and leave it unpicked.

*[Knocking at door]*

More knocking at the door? How now, what's the matter?

*[Enter BARDOLPH]*

BARDOLPH  You must away to court, sir, presently:
A dozen captains stay at door for you.
FALSTAFF  *[To Page]* Pay the musicians, sirrah. – Farewell, hostess,    305
farewell, Doll. You see, my good wenches, how men of merit are
sought after: the undeserver may sleep, when the man of action is
called on. Farewell, good wenches, if I be not sent away post, I will
see you again ere I go.
DOLL  I cannot speak. If my heart be not ready to burst – Well, sweet    310
Jack, have a care of thyself.
FALSTAFF  Farewell, farewell.

*Exit [with Bardolph, Page and Musicians]*

HOSTESS  Well, fare thee well. I have known thee these twenty-nine
years, come peascod time, but an honester and truer-hearted man
– Well, fare thee well.                                                  315
BARDOLPH  *[At the door]* Mistress Tearsheet!
HOSTESS  What's the matter?
BARDOLPH  Bid Mistress Tearsheet come to my master.
HOSTESS  O, run, Doll, run, run, good Doll! Come. – She comes
blubbered. – Yea, will you come Doll?                                    320

*Exeunt*

# Looking back at Act 2
*Activities for groups or individuals*

## 1 Scene openings

The opening 'business' (stage activity) of a scene can create atmosphere
and character before the first line is spoken. For example, one production
opened Scene 1 with Fang and Snare performing all kinds of marching
drills which demonstrated their incompetence.

Work out how to stage the openings of each scene in Act 2 to give an
unspoken indication of character or theme.

## 2 Women's point of view

All the female characters in the play appear in Act 2. In Shakespeare's
time, women's roles were acted by men (and as suggested on page 60
it is probable that the actors playing the Hostess and Doll doubled as
Lady Northumberland and Lady Percy).

What would happen if the two pairs of women met and exchanged
their views on all that has happened so far? What would they say to
each other? How much would their gender bond them together, and
their social class keep them apart? Work in a group of four, take parts
and tell each other what you think of the men and the events so far.

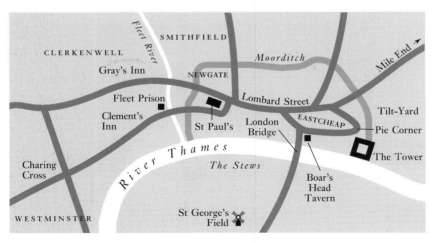

Falstaff's London. Make your own enlarged copy and illustrate it with
symbols and quotations.

## 3 Falstaff's relationships

Work in a pair and prepare a series of tableaux. Each of your frozen pictures shows Falstaff with a different character from Act 2 (Hostess, Lord Chief Justice, Doll, Prince Hal, Pistol, and so on). Show your tableaux to other pairs who guess which character is shown with Falstaff in each.

## 4 Poins

Poins is not an historical character but an invention of Shakespeare's. He seems to be a close friend of Prince Hal in *Parts 1* and *2*, but in both plays he disappears after Act 2. Who is he? In Scene 2, he describes himself as 'a second brother' and 'a proper fellow of my hands'. Write a list detailing all the things that would guide you if you were playing the part (biography, accent, costume, likes and dislikes, and so on).

## 5 Tavern sign

Design the inn sign that hangs outside the Boar's Head Tavern.

Doll, Falstaff, the Page and Pistol.
Find a line from Scene 4 as a suitable caption.

> *King Henry puzzles over why he is unable to sleep. He reflects that humble peasants and even a ship-boy in a terrible sea-storm can sleep, but a king, in the greatest comfort, cannot.*

## 1 Sleep (in small groups)

This is King Henry's first appearance in the play that bears his name. He is sick, his conscience troubles him, and he is unable to sleep, although it is after one o'clock in the morning. He reflects that whilst poor people, lying on uncomfortable straw beds ('uneasy pallets'), can sleep, a king's bed is like a 'watch-case, or a common 'larum bell' (a sentry box or alarm bell), places where sleep is forbidden.

Lines 4–31 are among the most famous in all Shakespeare. Prepare a delivery either by one speaker, or as a presentation on 'Sleep', spoken and enacted by several speakers who share out the lines, and speak as others mime some of the images.

## 2 'Uneasy lies the head …' (in small groups)

Take sides and argue for and against the claim that sleep is 'partial' (favouring the poor over the rich and powerful). Do kings, or anyone in a position of power, find it more difficult to sleep than ordinary people?

## 3 Personal experience?

One critic claimed that lines 20–5 show that Shakespeare himself had been caught in a storm at sea. What do you think? Give your own response to the claim that dramatists write best when they draw upon their own personal experience.

---

**steep** soak
**smoky cribs** chimneyless hovels
**costly state** expensive show
**the vile** low status people
**surge** ocean
**ruffian billows** dangerous waves

**hurly** uproar
**partial** biased
**sea-son** ship-boy
**all appliances … boot** everything that helps sleep
**happy low** contented peasants

# ACT 3 SCENE 1
## London: King Henry's palace

Enter the KING in his nightgown, alone with a Page

KING Go, call the Earls of Surrey and of Warwick;
But ere they come, bid them o'er-read these letters
And well consider of them. Make good speed.

*Exit [Page]*

How many thousand of my poorest subjects
Are at this hour asleep? O Sleep! O gentle Sleep!                    5
Nature's soft nurse, how have I frighted thee,
That thou no more wilt weigh my eye-lids down
And steep my senses in forgetfulness?
Why rather Sleep liest thou in smoky cribs,
Upon uneasy pallets stretching thee                                 10
And hushed with buzzing night-flies to thy slumber,
Than in the perfumed chambers of the great,
Under the canopies of costly state
And lulled with sound of sweetest melody?
O thou dull god, why liest thou with the vile,                      15
In loathsome beds, and leavest the kingly couch
A watch-case, or a common 'larum bell?
Wilt thou upon the high and giddy mast
Seal up the ship-boy's eyes and rock his brains
In cradle of the rude imperious surge                               20
And in the visitation of the winds,
Who take the ruffian billows by the top,
Curling their monstrous heads and hanging them
With deafing clamour in the slippery clouds,
That, with the hurly, death itself awakes?                          25
Canst thou, O partial Sleep, give thy repose
To the wet sea-son in an hour so rude,
And, in the calmest and most stillest night
With all appliances and means to boot,
Deny it to a king? Then happy low lie down,                         30
Uneasy lies the head that wears a crown.

*King Henry and Warwick compare England to a diseased human body.
Henry reflects that to foresee the future is to wish to die. He recalls how
King Richard and Northumberland, once friends, fought each other.*

## 1 Disease

In lines 37–43, King Henry and Warwick make a direct comparison
between a diseased human body and the rebellious state of the kingdom.
Who or what do you think they have in mind when they say 'heart'
(line 39) and 'medicine' (line 42)? Page 199 ('Imagery') can help you.

## 2 Sonnet 64: the effects of time

King Henry describes how the changes brought about by time ('the
revolution of the times') wear away mountains and alter coastlines as
sea and land encroach upon each other. His lines 45–50 echo
Shakespeare's Sonnet 64:

> When I have seen the hungry ocean gain
> Advantage on the Kingdom of the shore
> And the firm soil win of the wat'ry main,
> Increasing store with loss, and loss with store

Find a copy of Sonnet 64. Compare the meaning and mood of the
whole sonnet with lines 44–55.

## 3 Time and chance (in pairs)

Lines 50–2 contain a complex image of how the ironic jeering tricks of
fortune ('chance's mocks / And changes') bring about various ('divers')
changes in human lives. The image implies that men and women drink
from 'the cup of alteration'.

Suggest examples from real life of famous people who fall from their
position because of something unexpected. See also page 194.

---

rank  vile
distempered  sick
cooled  defeated
Neptune  Roman god of the sea
crosses to ensue  punishments to
  come

Percy  Northumberland
Nevil  Warwick
checked and rated  criticised and
  rebuked

*Enter* WARWICK *and* SURREY

WARWICK  Many good morrows to your majesty.
KING  Is it good morrow, lords?
WARWICK                               'Tis one o'clock, and past.
KING  Why then, good morrow to you all, my lords.
        Have you read o'er the letters that I sent you?          35
WARWICK  We have, my liege.
KING  Then you perceive the body of our kingdom
        How foul it is, what rank diseases grow,
        And with what danger near the heart of it.
WARWICK  It is but as a body yet distempered          40
        Which to his former strength may be restored
        With good advice and little medicine.
        My Lord Northumberland will soon be cooled.
KING  O God, that one might read the book of fate
        And see the revolution of the times          45
        Make mountains level, and the continent,
        Weary of solid firmness, melt itself
        Into the sea; and, other times, to see
        The beachy girdle of the ocean
        Too wide for Neptune's hips; how chance's mocks          50
        And changes fill the cup of alteration
        With divers liquors! O, if this were seen,
        The happiest youth, viewing his progress through,
        What perils past, what crosses to ensue,
        Would shut the book and sit him down and die.          55
        'Tis not ten years gone
        Since Richard and Northumberland, great friends,
        Did feast together; and in two year after
        Were they at wars. It is but eight years since
        This Percy was the man nearest my soul,          60
        Who like a brother toiled in my affairs
        And laid his love and life under my foot:
        Yea, for my sake, even to the eyes of Richard
        Gave him defiance. But which of you was by –
        You, cousin Nevil, as I may remember –          65
        When Richard, with his eye brimful of tears,
        Then checked and rated by Northumberland,
        Did speak these words, now proved a prophecy:

*King Henry recalls how King Richard prophesied civil war.*
*Warwick observes that history predicts future events, enabling King*
*Richard to foresee Northumberland's rebellion. Henry resolves to fight.*

## 1 Learning from history

In lines 56–78, King Henry recapitulates the story of how he came to
the throne. At the outset Northumberland (Percy) was his greatest ally
against King Richard II, who prophesied that Northumberland would
later rebel against Henry (see *Richard II* Act 5 Scene 1, lines 55–9).

Warwick reminds King Henry that lessons can be learned from
history. His lines 79–84 reflect a major belief of Shakespeare's time,
that a study of men's lives helps to predict the future, because the past
contains the seeds of the present and the future. Northumberland's
rebellion was predictable from his earlier behaviour.

Do you agree with Warwick that a study of history enables you to
predict the future? Give reasons for your reply.

## 2 'Necessity' (in small groups)

'Necessity' is a major theme of the play (see page 194). In lines 72, 86
and 91–2 'necessity' is used:

- to excuse Henry's action in seizing the crown of England
- to explain Northumberland's rebellion
- to guide future action.

Talk together about whether you think there are 'necessities' in
individual and social life: are certain happenings inevitable? Give
examples from your own experience.

## 3 Who was Glendower?

Glendower (line 102) was a Welsh prince, one of the rebels against
Henry in *Part 1*.

---

**Bullingbrook** King Henry
**amity** friendship
**Figuring ... times deceased**
 mirroring the past
**a near aim** accuracy
**main chance** probable outcomes
**intreasurèd** stored

**hatch and brood** children,
 hatched-out offspring
**necessary form** inevitable pattern
**cries out on us** spurs us on
**prize** victory
**unseasoned** late
**inward wars** civil wars

'Northumberland, thou ladder by the which
My cousin Bullingbrook ascends my throne'? –                    70
Though then, God knows, I had no such intent
But that necessity so bowed the state
That I and greatness were compelled to kiss. –
'The time shall come', thus did he follow it,
'The time will come that foul sin, gathering head,              75
Shall break into corruption.' So went on,
Foretelling this same time's condition
And the division of our amity.

WARWICK   There is a history in all men's lives
Figuring the natures of the times deceased,                     80
The which observed, a man may prophesy,
With a near aim, of the main chance of things
As yet not come to life, who in their seeds
And weak beginning lie intreasurèd.
Such things become the hatch and brood of time,                85
And by the necessary form of this
King Richard might create a perfect guess
That great Northumberland, then false to him,
Would of that seed grow to a greater falseness,
Which should not find a ground to root upon                     90
Unless on you.

KING                     Are these things then necessities?
Then let us meet them like necessities,
And that same word even now cries out on us.
They say the bishop and Northumberland
Are fifty thousand strong.

WARWICK                     It cannot be, my lord:               95
Rumour doth double, like the voice and echo,
The numbers of the feared. Please it your grace
To go to bed. Upon my soul, my lord,
The powers that you already have sent forth
Shall bring this prize in very easily.                          100
To comfort you the more, I have received
A certain instance that Glendower is dead.
Your majesty has been this fortnight ill,
And these unseasoned hours perforce must add
Unto your sickness.

KING                     I will take your counsel,               105
And were these inward wars once out of hand,
We would, dear lords, unto the Holy Land.        *Exeunt*

*Shallow questions Silence about his family, then reminisces about his own youthful experiences in London. He portrays himself as a devil-may-care and brave man-about-town in his youth.*

## 1 Shallow and Silence (in pairs)

Take parts, rehearse and act out lines 1–43. The director of one production wrote these notes for the actors:

> 'Here are two very old men, far from London, who live untroubled, comfortable lives on their estates, and who are local magistrates. They are both absolutely serious, they don't make jokes, but what they say can be very funny and very touching.
>
> Shallow looks back to a golden age when he was young. He portrays himself as a Jack-the-lad, a great fighter, drinker and womaniser who was friends with the great nobles of the day. None of it is true! He simply invents his own boastful and nostalgic version of his student days.
>
> Shallow's language has several features that an actor can exploit to great effect: he's a great repeater of words and phrases; he wanders from subject to subject, but he's got old age and death on his mind. He probably pauses a lot, seeming to forget what he wants to say, and he sometimes uses "a" for "he". In contrast, Silence says as little as possible!'

## 2 Possible reasons?

a Silence regretfully compares his daughter to a blackbird ('a black ousel'), perhaps because Queen Elizabeth's fair hair meant that black hair was no longer fashionable.

b In Shakespeare's time, the Inns of Court were law schools which acted as universities for the sons of aristocratic and well-to-do families. The four Inns of Court were highly fashionable, but Shallow attended Clement's Inn, which had lower status. Perhaps his awareness of its lower social esteem accounts for his boastfulness.

---

**early stirrer** early riser
**Rood** cross of Christ
**bedfellow** wife
**roundly** madly
**swinge-bucklers** swashbucklers
(shield beaters)

**bona robas** high-class prostitutes
**crack** young lad
**psalmist** the writer of Psalm 89 in
the Bible
**yoke** pair

# ACT 3    SCENE 2
## Gloucestershire: outside Justice Shallow's house

*Enter Justice* SHALLOW *and Justice* SILENCE

SHALLOW  Come on, come on, come on, sir, give me your hand, sir, give
me your hand, sir. An early stirrer, by the Rood! And how doth my
good cousin Silence?

SILENCE  Good morrow, good cousin Shallow.

SHALLOW  And how doth my cousin your bedfellow? And your fairest     5
daughter and mine, my god-daughter Ellen?

SILENCE  Alas, a black ousel, cousin Shallow.

SHALLOW  By yea and no, sir. I dare say my cousin William is become a
good scholar – he is at Oxford still, is he not?

SILENCE  Indeed, sir, to my cost.                                    10

SHALLOW  A must then to the Inns a'Court shortly. I was once at
Clement's Inn where I think they will talk of mad Shallow yet.

SILENCE  You were called Lusty Shallow then, cousin.

SHALLOW  By the Mass, I was called anything, and I would have done
anything indeed too, and roundly too. There was I, and little John   15
Doit of Staffordshire, and black George Barnes, and Francis
Pickbone, and Will Squele, a Cotswold man – you had not four such
swinge-bucklers in all the Inns a'Court again. And I may say to you
we knew where the bona robas were and had the best of them all at
commandment. Then was Jack Falstaff, now Sir John, a boy, and       20
page to Thomas Mowbray, Duke of Norfolk.

SILENCE  This Sir John, cousin, that comes hither anon about soldiers?

SHALLOW  The same Sir John, the very same. I see him break Scoggin's
head at the Court gate, when a was a crack not thus high; and the
very same day did I fight with one Samson Stockfish, a fruiterer,    25
behind Gray's Inn. Jesu, Jesu, the mad days that I have spent! And
to see how many of my old acquaintance are dead.

SILENCE  We shall all follow, cousin.

SHALLOW  Certain, 'tis certain, very sure, very sure. Death, as the
psalmist saith, is certain to all, all shall die. How a good yoke of  30
bullocks at Stamford Fair?

*Shallow recalls that old Dooble was, in his youth, an excellent bowman.*
*His mind wanders to the price of sheep then back to thoughts of death.*
*He is fascinated by Bardolph's word 'accommodated'.*

## 1 Justice Shallow, Esquire (in pairs)

Further aspects of Justice Shallow emerge. He likes using technical language about archery. His social status is 'esquire', a rank just below that of knight. He is a justice of the peace: a law officer who acted as judge for his local area.

Like many Elizabethans of his social rank in Shakespeare's time, Shallow takes a lively interest in language. Bardolph uses a word that takes Shallow's fancy – 'accommodated' – which Bardolph uses to mean 'provided'. Shallow rolls it around his tongue, and explains its Latin origin. He uses, in his turn, a word that is unfamiliar to Bardolph: 'phrase'. Bardolph feels that he has to explain 'accommodated', but finishes up saying it means just that – 'accommodated'.

Explore ways of staging the dialogue between Bardolph and Shallow (lines 45–65) to show Shallow's pride in his social position, his delight in hearing a new word, and Bardolph's attempt to define 'accommodated'.

## 2 Who is it?

The stage direction at line 44 says that Bardolph enters 'and one with him'. The other person does not speak in the scene. Suggest what reason Shakespeare might have had in mind for including this silent character. Then suggest, if you were directing the play, who you would bring on to accompany Bardolph and what that silent character might do.

---

**By my troth** in truth
**John a'Gaunt** Henry IV's father
**clapped i'th'clout** hit the centre
of the target
**twelve score** 240 yards
**forehand shaft** heavy arrow for
straight shooting

**fourteen and a half** 290 yards
**How a score of ewes, ...?** what's
the price of twenty sheep?
**Thereafter as they be** depending
on their condition
**backsword** stick with basket work
hilt, used to practise sword-fencing

SILENCE  By my troth, I was not there.

SHALLOW  Death is certain. Is old Dooble of your town living yet?

SILENCE  Dead, sir.

SHALLOW  Jesu, Jesu, dead! A drew a good bow, and dead! A shot a fine     35
shoot. John a'Gaunt loved him well and betted much money on his
head. Dead! A would have clapped i'th'clout at twelve score, and
carried you a forehand shaft a fourteen and fourteen and a half, that
it would have done a man's heart good to see. How a score of ewes,
now?     40

SILENCE  Thereafter as they be: a score of good ewes may be worth ten
pounds.

SHALLOW  And is old Dooble dead?

SILENCE  Here come two of Sir John Falstaff's men, as I think.

*Enter* BARDOLPH *and one with him*

Good morrow, honest gentlemen.     45

BARDOLPH  I beseech you, which is Justice Shallow?

SHALLOW  I am Robert Shallow, sir, a poor esquire of this county, and
one of the king's justices of the peace. What is your good pleasure
with me?

BARDOLPH  My captain, sir, commends him to you, my captain Sir John     50
Falstaff, a tall gentleman, by heaven, and a most gallant leader.

SHALLOW  He greets me well, sir; I knew him a good backsword man.
How doth the good knight? May I ask how my lady his wife doth?

BARDOLPH  Sir, pardon, a soldier is better accommodated than with a
wife.     55

SHALLOW  It is well said, in faith, sir, and it is well said indeed too: 'better
accommodated'! It is good, yea indeed is it. Good phrases are surely,
and ever were, very commendable. 'Accommodated': it comes of
*accommodo*. Very good, a good phrase.

BARDOLPH  Pardon, sir, I have heard the word – phrase call you it? By this     60
day, I know not the phrase, but I will maintain the word with my
sword to be a soldierlike word, and a word of exceeding good
command, by heaven. Accommodated, that is when a man is, as they
say, accommodated, or when a man is being whereby a may be
thought to be accommodated, which is an excellent thing.     65

*Shallow welcomes Falstaff, and the process of recruiting begins. Falstaff jokes about Mouldy's name. Mouldy protests that he cannot leave his wife and the work she needs done.*

## 1 'Master Soccard'

In one early version of the play, Falstaff calls Silence 'Surecard', not Soccard. No one knows what 'Soccard' might mean, but 'Surecard' can suggest some meanings (for example, 'certain to win', 'good player'). If you were playing Falstaff would you use 'Soccard' or 'Surecard'? Give a reason for your decision.

## 2 Stage the recruiting scene (in groups of eight)

Lines 75–244 show Falstaff recruiting his soldiers. Take parts and rehearse the episode. If you have limited time, you could choose a shorter version, lines 75–157, which show Falstaff interviewing the recruits, and lines 198–221 which show how he makes his selection.

Each recruit can invent an appropriate entry, style of speaking, and so on for their character. Bardolph might escort every recruit.

The stage direction requires all five recruits to appear together at line 81. But in some productions the five recruits enter at the start of the scene. In others they enter one by one as they are called by name (lines 81–144). Think about the dramatic effect of all three possibilities, then decide which you would use to stage the entry of the recruits.

## 3 Recruiting methods

See page 104 for information on recruiting methods.

---

**in commission** acting as a justice of the peace
**sufficient** fit for military service
**roll** list of recruits

**Prick him** mark him down on the list
**dame** wife
**husbandry** farm work
**spent** used

*Enter Sir John* FALSTAFF

SHALLOW  It is very just. – Look, here comes good Sir John. Give me your good hand, give me your worship's good hand. By my troth, you like well and bear your years very well. Welcome, good Sir John.

FALSTAFF  I am glad to see you well, good Master Robert Shallow. Master Soccard, as I think.                                                              70

SHALLOW  No, Sir John, it is my cousin Silence, in commission with me.

FALSTAFF  Good Master Silence, it well befits you should be of the peace.

SILENCE  Your good worship is welcome.

FALSTAFF  Fie, this is hot weather, gentlemen. Have you provided me    75
here half a dozen sufficient men?

SHALLOW  Marry have we, sir. Will you sit?

FALSTAFF  Let me see them, I beseech you.

SHALLOW  Where's the roll, where's the roll, where's the roll? Let me see, let me see, let me see. So, so, so, so, so. So, so, yea marry, sir. – Rafe    80
Mouldy! – Let them appear as I call, let them do so, let them do so.

[*Enter* MOULDY, SHADOW, WART, FEEBLE, BULLCALF]

Let me see, where is Mouldy?

MOULDY  Here, and't please you.

SHALLOW  What think you, Sir John, a good-limbed fellow, young, strong, and of good friends.                                                          85

FALSTAFF  Is thy name Mouldy?

MOULDY  Yea, and't please you.

FALSTAFF  'Tis the more time thou wert used.

SHALLOW  Ha, ha, ha, most excellent, i'faith. Things that are mouldy lack use, very singular good, in faith. Well said, Sir John, very well said.    90

FALSTAFF  Prick him.

MOULDY  I was pricked well enough before, and you could have let me alone. My old dame will be undone now for one to do her husbandry and her drudgery. You need not to have pricked me: there are other men fitter to go out than I.                                                         95

FALSTAFF  Go to; peace, Mouldy, you shall go, Mouldy, it is time you were spent.

MOULDY  Spent?

SHALLOW  Peace, fellow, peace, stand aside: know you where you are? – For th'other, Sir John. Let me see – Simon Shadow!                             100

*Falstaff jokes about Shadow's name, implying that Shadow has no legitimate father. Wart is rejected, but Falstaff praises Feeble and selects him.*

Falstaff selects his recruits.

## 1 'Shadows fill up the muster-book'

Corrupt officers like Falstaff often invented fictitious names ('shadows') to make up the number of their regiments. They received money from the king's exchequer for each name, and would pocket the pay of the non-existent soldiers.

Each regiment kept a muster-book: a book recording the names and personal details of each soldier. The officer probably had a secret code, known only to himself, to show which soldiers were real, and which were 'shadows'.

Write out a page of Falstaff's muster-book to show actual soldiers and 'shadows'.

---

**superfluous** unnecessary
**for his apparel ... pins** his
  clothes and body look as if they are
  held together with pins

**magnanimous** stout-hearted
**many thousands** (of lice)

FALSTAFF  Yea marry, let me have him to sit under: he's like to be a cold
  soldier.

SHALLOW  Where's Shadow?

SHADOW  Here, sir.

FALSTAFF  Shadow, whose son art thou?                                    105

SHADOW  My mother's son, sir.

FALSTAFF  Thy mother's son! Like enough, and thy father's shadow: so
  the son of the female is the shadow of the male. It is often so indeed
  – but much of the father's substance!

SHALLOW  Do you like him, Sir John?                                       110

FALSTAFF  Shadow will serve for summer: prick him, for we have a
  number of shadows fill up the muster-book.

SHALLOW  Thomas Wart!

FALSTAFF  Where's he?

WART  Here, sir.                                                         115

FALSTAFF  Is thy name Wart?

WART  Yea, sir.

FALSTAFF  Thou art a very ragged Wart.

SHALLOW  Shall I prick him, Sir John?

FALSTAFF  It were superfluous, for his apparel is built upon his back, and   120
  the whole frame stands upon pins. Prick him no more.

SHALLOW  Ha, ha, ha, you can do it, sir, you can do it, I commend you
  well. – Francis Feeble!

FEEBLE  Here, sir.

SHALLOW  What trade art thou, Feeble?                                    125

FEEBLE  A woman's tailor, sir.

SHALLOW  Shall I prick him, sir?

FALSTAFF  You may, but if he had been a man's tailor, he'd ha'pricked
  you. Wilt thou make as many holes in an enemy's battle as thou hast
  done in a woman's petticoat?                                           130

FEEBLE  I will do my good will, sir, you can have no more.

FALSTAFF  Well said, good woman's tailor, well said, courageous Feeble.
  Thou wilt be as valiant as the wrathful dove or most magnanimous
  mouse. Prick the woman's tailor well, Master Shallow, deep,
  Master Shallow.                                                        135

FEEBLE  I would Wart might have gone, sir.

FALSTAFF  I would thou wert a man's tailor, that thou mightst mend him
  and make him fit to go. I cannot put him to a private soldier, that is the
  leader of so many thousands. Let that suffice, most forcible Feeble.

FEEBLE  It shall suffice, sir.                                           140

*Falstaff recruits the unwilling Bullcalf. Shallow recalls the long ago days in London when he and Falstaff were young men. Falstaff's words are a reminder of their late-night roistering.*

## 1 A change of mood (in groups of three)

Lines 160–80 mark a change of mood in Scene 2. In many productions, directors seize the opportunity to create a feeling of nostalgia and longing, as both men look back fifty-five years to their youth to remember their high jinks as students in London. To increase dramatic effect, the lines are sometimes played very slowly with long pauses, and with lighting changes to create an autumnal, melancholy mood.

Falstaff's line 177 'We have heard the chimes at midnight' has become well known to express recollection in old age of the high-spirited adventures of youth. Orson Welles used it as the title of his film about Falstaff, *Chimes at Midnight*. The film opens with Falstaff, old and weary, sheltering in the windmill in Saint George's Field.

In contrast to the elegiac mood often portrayed, one production showed Falstaff watching Shallow with evident impatience and distaste. He was clearly thinking 'I wish the old fool would stop maundering on'. His replies to Shallow were terse and barely courteous, only just concealing his impatience. He spoke his famous line 177 as a flat, unemphatic and unenthusiastic confirmation of Shallow's claims, showing clearly to the audience that he simply doesn't believe it.

How would you stage lines 160–80? Take parts as Falstaff, Shallow and Silence and experiment with different styles to create different moods.

## 2 How old is Falstaff?

Use lines 20 and 174 to work out approximately the ages of Shallow and Falstaff.

---

**ringing** bell-ringing (the king's coronation was celebrated each year with bell-ringing)

**in a gown** dressing gown (as a sign of sickness)

**ring for thee** ring in your place, ring for your funeral

**Windmill in Saint George's Field** a windmill or brothel in Southwark (see map on page 80)

**'Hem, boys'** a drinking toast (like 'cheers!')

FALSTAFF  I am bound to thee, reverend Feeble. – Who is next?

SHALLOW  Peter Bullcalf o'th'Green.

FALSTAFF  Yea marry, let's see Bullcalf.

BULLCALF  Here, sir.

FALSTAFF  'Fore God, a likely fellow. Come, prick Bullcalf till he roar  145
again.

BULLCALF  O Lord, good my lord captain.

FALSTAFF  What, dost thou roar before thou art pricked?

BULLCALF  O Lord, sir, I am a diseased man.

FALSTAFF  What disease hast thou?  150

BULLCALF  A whoreson cold, sir, a cough, sir, which I caught with
ringing in the king's affairs upon his coronation day, sir.

FALSTAFF  Come, thou shalt go to the wars in a gown; we will have away
thy cold and I will take such order that thy friends shall ring for thee.
– Is here all?  155

SHALLOW  Here is two more called than your number: you must have but
four here, sir, and so I pray you go in with me to dinner.

FALSTAFF  Come, I will go drink with you, but I cannot tarry dinner. I am
glad to see you, by my troth, Master Shallow.

SHALLOW  O Sir John, do you remember since we lay all night in the  160
Windmill in Saint George's Field?

FALSTAFF  No more of that, Master Shallow.

SHALLOW  Ha, 'twas a merry night. And is Jane Nightwork alive?

FALSTAFF  She lives, Master Shallow.

SHALLOW  She never could away with me.  165

FALSTAFF  Never never, she would always say she could not abide Master
Shallow.

SHALLOW  By the Mass, I could anger her to th'heart. She was then a
bona roba; doth she hold her own well?

FALSTAFF  Old, old, Master Shallow.  170

SHALLOW  Nay, she must be old, she cannot choose but be old; certain
she's old, and had Robin Nightwork by old Nightwork, before I
came to Clement's Inn.

SILENCE  That's fifty-five year ago.

SHALLOW  Ha, cousin Silence, that thou hadst seen that that this knight  175
and I have seen! Ha, Sir John, said I well?

FALSTAFF  We have heard the chimes at midnight, Master Shallow.

SHALLOW  That we have, that we have, that we have in faith, Sir John, we
have. Our watchword was 'Hem, boys.' Come let's to dinner, come
let's to dinner. Jesus, the days that we have seen! Come, come.  180

*Exeunt [Falstaff, Shallow and Silence]*

*Bullcalf and Mouldy bribe Bardolph to release them from recruitment. Feeble declares he will serve as a soldier. Falstaff, told by Bardolph of the bribes, releases Mouldy and Bullcalf. Shallow protests.*

## 1 Bribing Bardolph (in small groups)

Work out how to stage the bribing episode in lines 181–97. Bardolph has probably guarded and guided the recruits throughout Falstaff's questioning. Now he is left alone with them. In some productions, he approaches each recruit with a significant look, obviously inviting a bribe. In others, the recruits approach Bardolph.

What do Bullcalf and Mouldy do on Bardolph's command, 'Go to, stand aside'?

## 2 Francis Feeble

Women's tailors were stereotyped in Elizabethan times as natural cowards. Falstaff has joked about Feeble's bravery in lines 132–4. Now Feeble shows he really has more courage than Bullcalf or Mouldy.

Remind yourself of how Feeble replied to Falstaff (lines 126–40) and speak Feeble's lines opposite in a style you feel is appropriate to his character.

## 3 How much?

Does Bardolph cheat Falstaff? Bardolph tells Falstaff that he has received three pounds in bribes. He might have actually received £4 because Bullcalf's 'four Harry ten shillings' could be worth £1 or £2 depending on whether it was calculated in Shakespeare's time or King Henry IV's time.

If you were directing the play, would you want to show Bardolph pocketing an extra £1 for himself? Which possibility seems most in character, and most dramatically effective to you?

---

**Corporate** corporal
**four Harry ten shillings** worth
£1 in total
**as lief** rather

**old dame's** wife's
**forty** forty shillings, £2
**is quit** owes nothing

BULLCALF  Good Master Corporate Bardolph, stand my friend, and here's four Harry ten shillings in French crowns for you. In very truth, sir, I had as lief be hanged, sir, as go; and yet for mine own part, sir, I do not care, but rather because I am unwilling, and for mine own part have a desire to stay with my friends; else, sir, I did     185
not care for mine own part so much.

BARDOLPH  Go, to, stand aside.

MOULDY  And good master corporal captain, for my old dame's sake, stand my friend: she has nobody to do anything about her when I am gone, and she is old and cannot help herself. You shall have forty, sir.     190

BARDOLPH  Go to, stand aside.

FEEBLE  By my troth, I care not, a man can die but once: we owe God a death. I'll ne'er bear a base mind; and't be my destiny, so; and't be not, so. No man's too good to serve's prince, and let it go which way it will, he that dies this year is quit for the next.     195

BARDOLPH  Well said, th'art a good fellow.

FEEBLE  Faith, I'll bear no base mind.

*Enter* FALSTAFF *and the* JUSTICES

FALSTAFF  Come, sir, which men shall I have?

SHALLOW  Four of which you please.

BARDOLPH  Sir, a word with you: I have three pound to free Mouldy and     200
Bullcalf.

FALSTAFF  Go to, well.

SHALLOW  Come, Sir John, which four will you have?

FALSTAFF  Do you choose for me.

SHALLOW  Marry then, Mouldy, Bullcalf, Feeble and Shadow.     205

FALSTAFF  Mouldy and Bullcalf: for you, Mouldy, stay at home till you are past service; and for your part, Bullcalf, grow till you come unto it. I will none of you.

SHALLOW  Sir John, Sir John, do not yourself wrong: they are your likeliest men, and I would have you served with the best.     210

*Falstaff's explanation of how he chose his soldiers is a parody of military
selection criteria. Bardolph directs Wart at arms drill, prompting
Shallow to recall his own experience.*

## 1 What can Wart do?

Falstaff claims that Wart can load and fire his musket like lightning
('with the motion of a pewterer's hammer': pewter was beaten into
shape with rapid blows). But no one is quite sure what Falstaff means
by 'come off and on swifter than he that gibbets on the brewer's
bucket'. Perhaps the image is of raising and lowering a musket very
quickly, like a barman who carries two buckets of beer on a yoke across
his shoulders. One student suggested that Falstaff has in mind that
Wart will die very quickly in battle ('kick the bucket').

Make your own suggestion and invent stage business to demonstrate it.

## 2 Arms drill (in small groups)

Bardolph puts Wart through his musket drill like a sergeant major
barking orders at a recruit (line 222). Shallow does not think much of
Wart's performance, and recollects seeing 'a little quiver fellow'
performing musket drill over fifty years ago.

Invent your own actions for Wart and Shallow to perform. Does one
of them threaten to shoot the audience at some point? Use the following
to help you with lines 230–1:

'manage you his piece' – Hold his musket.

'about and about' – Musketeers stood in ranks. The first would
fire, then step back behind the rear rank to reload.

'come you in' – Each rank then fired in turn and stepped
back to reload.

'Rah, tah, tah!' – Spoken by the musketeer as he reloaded,
ramming the musket ball into the muzzle.

'Bounce' – Bang.

---

**thews** muscles
**assemblance** appearance
**charge ... discharge** load and fire
**caliver** small musket
**Traverse!** change your aim!
**tester** sixpence

**Sir Dagonet in Arthur's show**
 the fool in an archery pageant
**quiver** nimble
**piece** musket
**coats** cheap uniforms
**Peradventure** perhaps (How does
 Shallow speak line 240?)

FALSTAFF Will you tell me, Master Shallow, how to choose a man? Care I for the limb, the thews, the stature, bulk, and big assemblance of a man? Give me the spirit, Master Shallow. Here's Wart: you see what a ragged appearance it is. A shall charge you and discharge you with the motion of a pewterer's hammer: come off and on swifter 215 than he that gibbets on the brewer's bucket. And this same half-faced fellow, Shadow: give me this man. He presents no mark to the enemy, the foeman may with as great aim level at the edge of a penknife. And for a retreat, how swiftly will this Feeble, the woman's tailor, run off! O, give me the spare men, and spare me the 220 great ones. – Put me a caliver into Wart's hand, Bardolph.

BARDOLPH Hold, Wart! Traverse! Thas, thas, thas!

FALSTAFF Come, manage me your caliver: so, very well, go to, very good, exceeding good. O, give me always a little, lean, old, chopped, bald shot. Well said, i'faith, Wart. Th'art a good scab. Hold, there's a 225 tester for you.

SHALLOW He is not his craft's master, he doth not do it right. I remember at Mile End Green, when I lay at Clement's Inn – I was then Sir Dagonet in Arthur's show – there was a little quiver fellow and a would manage you his piece thus, and a would about and about, and 230 come you in, and come you in. 'Rah, tah, tah!' would a say; 'Bounce' would a say, and away again would a go, and again would a come. I shall ne'er see such a fellow.

FALSTAFF These fellows will do well, Master Shallow. God keep you, Master Silence, I will not use many words with you. Fare you well, 235 gentlemen both, I thank you. I must a dozen mile tonight. Bardolph, give the soldiers coats.

SHALLOW Sir John, the Lord bless you, God prosper your affairs, God send us peace. At your return visit our house, let our old acquaintance be renewed. Peradventure I will with ye to the court. 240

*Falstaff resolves to visit Shallow again and trick him out of his money. He mocks Shallow's lying about his youthful exploits, and describes the young Shallow's skinny appearance and foolish behaviour.*

## 1 Falstaff's real thoughts (in pairs)

Falstaff's soliloquy reveals as much about himself as it does about Justice Shallow. He intends to cheat ('fetch off') Shallow. Like an old pike, he will gobble up the young dace (small fish used as bait).

Rehearse a delivery of his lines thinking about whether he stands or sits, speaks directly to the audience or to himself, pauses lengthily at certain points as he recalls Shallow's behaviour, and so on. Also consider what 'business' he might use. (In one production he held a large tankard and drank from it thro.ughout the soliloquy.) Is his mocking of Shallow affectionate, or contemptuous, or ...?

## 2 Remembering Shallow

Falstaff considers Shallow to be an out-and-out liar about his youth, remembering him as a skinny nonentity who was always behind the fashion as he tried to impress worn-out prostitutes ('overscutched housewives').

What was Shallow really like? Step into role as one of the characters named in lines 15–17 (John Doit, George Barnes, Francis Pickbone, Will Squele) who were at Clement's Inn with him. Tell your story of Robert Shallow – and John Falstaff!

## 3 Leaving the stage

Write notes to guide the actors as to how they should leave the stage at lines 243, 244 and 269. Give each man a gesture or action to signify his character.

---

**Turnbull Street** brothel area in Clerkenwell
**duer** more quickly
**Turk's tribute** tributes to the Turkish sultan had to be paid quickly on pain of death
**mandrake** plant used as aphrodisiac

**carmen** carters
**Vice** character in old Morality play
**tilt-yard** jousting arena
**marshal** master of ceremonies
**treble hautboy** slender oboe
**philosopher's two stones** goldmine (like stones that can turn anything to gold)

FALSTAFF  'Fore God, would you would.
SHALLOW  Go to, I have spoke at a word. God keep you.
FALSTAFF  Fare you well, gentlemen.

*Exeunt [Shallow and Silence]*

On, Bardolph, lead the men away.

*[Exeunt Bardolph and the rest]*

As I return, I will fetch off these justices. I do see the bottom of    245
Justice Shallow. Lord, Lord, how subject we old men are to this
vice of lying! This same starved justice hath done nothing but prate
to me of the wildness of his youth and the feats he hath done about
Turnbull Street, and every third word a lie, duer paid to the hearer
than the Turk's tribute. I do remember him at Clement's Inn, like    250
a man made after supper of a cheese-paring. When a was naked, he
was, for all the world, like a forked radish, with a head fantastically
carved upon it with a knife. A was so forlorn that his dimensions to
any thick sight were invincible. A was the very genius of famine,
yet lecherous as a monkey and the whores called him mandrake. A    255
came ever in the rearward of the fashion, and sung those tunes to
the overscutched housewives that he heard the carmen whistle,
and swear they were his fancies or his good-nights. And now is this
Vice's dagger become a squire, and talks as familiarly of John
a'Gaunt as if he had been sworn brother to him, and I'll be sworn a    260
ne'er saw him but once in the tilt-yard, and then he burst his head
for crowding among the marshal's men. I saw it and told John
a'Gaunt he beat his own name, for you might have thrust him and
all his apparel into an eel-skin: the case of a treble hautboy was a
mansion for him, a court; and now has he land and beefs. Well, I'll    265
be acquainted with him if I return, and't shall go hard but I'll make
him a philosopher's two stones to me. If the young dace be a bait for
the old pike, I see no reason in the law of nature but I may snap at
him. Let time shape, and there an end.

*Exit*

# Looking back at Act 3
*Activities for groups or individuals*

## 1 Falstaff, King Henry and England

Act 3 opens with Henry's soliloquy on how the cares of kingship prevent sleep, and closes with Falstaff's soliloquy on Justice Shallow and plans to cheat him. Work out a presentation of both speeches which brings out the differences between the two men, and which reveals something about the nature of Henry's England. You might, for example, experiment with intercutting some of the lines of the two soliloquies.

## 2 The 'King's Press'

Scene 2 exposes how corrupt officers in Shakespeare's time abused the 'King's Press' (the system by which soldiers were recruited). Each Justice of the Peace was required to provide a number of fit men for the recruiting officer to interview. The officer questioned each man, and when he selected a recruit, ordered 'Prick him' (place a mark alongside his name on the list).

To avoid being 'pricked', men offered bribes to the recruiting officer to excuse them from selection. Such bribes made the officer rich, and he selected only the poorest recruits who could not afford to bribe their way out of military service. In *Henry IV Part 1*, Falstaff describes his recruiting methods and its results:

> 'If I be not ashamed of my soldiers, I am a soused gurnet. I have misused the King's press damnably. I have got, in exchange of a hundred and fifty soldiers, three hundred and odd pounds.'

a Step into role as one of Falstaff's recruits. Tell your own story of what happens in Scene 2.

b Is Falstaff a likeable jolly fat man, a nasty racketeer, or ...?
  Imagine you are directing the play. What emotions would you wish an audience to feel towards Falstaff during the recruiting scene?

## 3 Themes

Turn to pages 190–4 and remind yourself of some major themes of the play. Then identify several ways in which Scenes 1 and 2 express those themes: for example, order and disorder; sickness and disease in individuals and society; time; 'Policy' (deceit), and so on.

'Welcome, good Sir John.' Falstaff is greeted by Justice Shallow. Do you think that Falstaff's face shows his intention to defraud Shallow?

## 4 Poor geography?

Falstaff is on his way from London to Gaultree Forest in Yorkshire. Look at the map on page 2, then answer the following question, first as Shakespeare, second as Falstaff: 'What is Falstaff doing in Gloucestershire?'

*The Archbishop reports that Northumberland is unable to raise an army suitable to his rank. He sends only his good wishes. The Messenger brings news that the king's army is only a mile away.*

## 1 Design the set

Scene 1 is set in the forest of Gaultree. It was an ancient forest ten miles north of the city of York (but was cleared in the century after Shakespeare). In this scene, it will be the setting of an act of cold betrayal.

In Shakespeare's theatre, where the action of the play flowed continuously, the scene was played on a bare stage, or with a minimum of props to signify the forest. A modern theatre has far more resources to help create atmosphere and location.

Design a simple set, and suggest lighting and sound effects that will express the sombre nature of the forest to the audience.

## 2 Northumberland's letters (in pairs)

Northumberland will not join the rebels to fight against King Henry. He once again defects, just as he did in *Part 1*, where he failed to join his son Hotspur at the Battle of Shrewsbury. Now he sends only 'hearty prayers' for his fellow rebels' success.

a Take turns to speak the Archbishop's lines 6–16 in a tone that displays his attitude to Northumberland's news.

b Write one of Northumberland's letters. You will find it helpful to remind yourself of what was said in Act 2 Scene 3, where Northumberland took the decision to go to Scotland, rather than join the Archbishop's forces.

discoverers scouts
tenor meaning
hold sortance ... quality be
  appropriate to his high status

levy recruit
ripe extend, increase
opposites adversaries (King
  Henry's army, led by Prince John)

# ACT 4  SCENE 1
## The forest of Gaultree

*Enter the* ARCHBISHOP *of York,* MOWBRAY *and* HASTINGS

ARCHBISHOP  What is this forest called?

HASTINGS  'Tis Gaultree forest, and't shall please your grace.

ARCHBISHOP  Here stand, my lords, and send discoverers forth
 To know the numbers of our enemies.

HASTINGS  We have sent forth already.

ARCHBISHOP                          'Tis well done.          5
 My friends and brethren in these great affairs,
 I must acquaint you that I have received
 New-dated letters from Northumberland;
 Their cold intent, tenor and substance thus:
 Here doth he wish his person, with such powers          10
 As might hold sortance with his quality,
 The which he could not levy, whereupon
 He is retired to ripe his growing fortunes
 To Scotland; and concludes in hearty prayers
 That your attempts may overlive the hazard          15
 And fearful meeting of their opposites.

MOWBRAY  Thus do the hopes we have in him touch ground
 And dash themselves to pieces.

*Enter a* MESSENGER

HASTINGS                          Now, what news?

MESSENGER  West of this forest, scarcely off a mile,
 In goodly form comes on the enemy,          20
 And, by the ground they hide, I judge their number
 Upon or near the rate of thirty thousand.

*Mowbray urges instant battle. Westmoreland tells the Archbishop that rebellion is naturally led by wild youths and beggars, not noblemen. He asks why the Archbishop has turned from peace to war.*

## 1 Rebellion (in pairs)

**a** In lines 32–41, Westmoreland uses many negative words to describe rebellion (for example, 'abject routs' are despicable mobs). He balances them with positive words to describe the rebels. Speak his lines (from 'If that' to 'fair honours'), emphasising the positive and negative words in very different ways.

**b** In lines 41–52 ('You, Lord Archbishop ... point of war?'), Westmoreland speaks directly to the Archbishop. He again balances good qualities against bad, positive against negative. He also uses repetition, both of individual words ('Whose') and the rhythm of lines. Take turns to speak the lines as persuasively as you can, bringing out the balance between peace and war.

## 2 Rebels or freedom fighters? (in small groups)

Westmoreland claims that his description of a mob of beggars and angry youths shows rebellion's 'true, native and most proper shape', and its essence ('like itself'). But he does not mention that his own leader, now King Henry IV, was himself once a rebel, overthrowing King Richard II.

When does an army of 'rebels' become an army of 'freedom fighters'? Brainstorm examples of 'rebellion': they can be from history or from personal experience. Then consider each in turn, deciding who calls who a 'rebel'. Do the rebels think of themselves as rebels – or freedom fighters? From your practical examples try to decide whether there is (as Westmoreland claims) such a thing as the 'true, native and most proper shape' of rebellion.

---

**just proportion ... out** precise number that we guessed
**sway on** advance
**countenanced** cheered on
**commotion** rebellion
**see** diocese
**good letters** scholarship

**investments** robes (high-ranking churchmen always wore white, even when they were part of an army)
**figure** symbolise
**ill translate** wrongly transform
**point of war** trumpet call

MOWBRAY  The just proportion that we gave them out.
        Let us sway on and face them in the field.

        *Enter* WESTMORELAND

ARCHBISHOP  What well-appointed leader fronts us here?                    25
MOWBRAY  I think it is my Lord of Westmoreland.
WESTMORELAND  Health and fair greeting from our general,
        The prince Lord John and Duke of Lancaster.
ARCHBISHOP  Say on, my Lord of Westmoreland, in peace,
        What doth concern your coming.
WESTMORELAND                          Then, my lord,                     30
        Unto your grace do I in chief address
        The substance of my speech. If that rebellion
        Came like itself in base and abject routs
        Led on by bloody youth, guarded with rage,
        And countenanced by boys and beggary –                           35
        I say, if damned commotion so appear
        In his true, native and most proper shape,
        You, reverend father, and these noble lords
        Had not been here to dress the ugly form
        Of base and bloody insurrection                                  40
        With your fair honours. You, Lord Archbishop,
        Whose see is by a civil peace maintained,
        Whose beard the silver hand of peace hath touched,
        Whose learning and good letters peace hath tutored,
        Whose white investments figure innocence,                        45
        The dove and very blessed spirit of peace,
        Wherefore do you so ill translate yourself
        Out of the speech of peace, that bears such grace,
        Into the harsh and boist'rous tongue of war –
        Turning your books to graves, your ink to blood,                 50
        Your pens to lances and your tongue divine
        To a loud trumpet and a point of war?

*The Archbishop claims that the corrupt state of England makes him lead
the rebellion. He has been prevented from presenting the rebels'
grievances to the king. His intention is to establish peace.*

## 1 'We are all diseased' (in pairs)

The Archbishop will wish to present his reasons for rebellion as
persuasively as possible. Take turns to speak his lines to make them as
convincing as you can. Keep in mind that he is a churchman, not a
soldier. The following can help your delivery of the speech.

In lines 53–66, the Archbishop likens England to a sick person. In
Elizabethan times, doctors attempted to cure many diseases by bleeding
(letting some blood drain from the patient), by purging (giving
unpleasant medicines), and by dieting ('diet rank minds' implies
punishing corrupt people). The cure for England's sickness, the
Archbishop argues, is the bloodletting and purging of war. He goes on
to claim that the rebels have been prevented by corrupt people from
presenting their list of grievances to King Henry.

## 2 'We': who? (in pairs)

The actor playing the Archbishop says to you:

'I have a problem with the pronouns! Just who is the Archbishop talking
about when he uses "we" and "our"? Does he mean the rebels, or
everyone in England, or himself?'

Work through the Archbishop's speech and suggest who he has in
mind at each 'we' and 'our'.

## 3 'The rough torrent of occasion'

For information on how politics is about responding to events, see page
194 ('rough torrent of occasion' means force of circumstance, or
events).

---

**surfeiting and wanton hours**
  riotous living
**Troop** march, fight
**most quiet** peace
**articles** a list of grievances,
  a petition
**suit** pleading

**gain our audience** speak with
  the king
**Of every minute's instance**
  occuring every minute
**ill-beseeming arms** unsuitable
  armour

ARCHBISHOP  Wherefore do I this? So the question stands.
Briefly, to this end: we are all diseased,
And with our surfeiting and wanton hours                    55
Have brought ourselves into a burning fever
And we must bleed for it; of which disease
Our late King Richard being infected died.
But, my most noble Lord of Westmoreland,
I take not on me here as a physician,                       60
Nor do I, as an enemy to peace,
Troop in the throngs of military men,
But rather show a while like fearful war
To diet rank minds, sick of happiness,
And purge th'obstructions which begin to stop              65
Our very veins of life. Hear me more plainly:
I have in equal balance justly weighed
What wrongs our arms may do, what wrongs we suffer,
And find our griefs heavier than our offences.
We see which way the stream of time doth run               70
And are enforced from our most quiet there
By the rough torrent of occasion,
And have the summary of all our griefs,
When time shall serve, to show in articles
Which long ere this we offered to the king                 75
And might by no suit gain our audience.
When we are wronged and would unfold our griefs
We are denied access unto his person
Even by those men that most have done us wrong.
The dangers of the days but newly gone,                    80
Whose memory is written on the earth
With yet-appearing blood, and the examples
Of every minute's instance, present now,
Hath put us in these ill-beseeming arms,
Not to break peace or any branch of it,                    85
But to establish here a peace indeed
Concurring both in name and quality.

*The Archbishop gives two reasons for his rebellion: the common good and his brother's death. Mowbray recalls that his father was once about to fight Bullingbrook when King Richard intervened.*

## 1 Reasons for rebellion

The Archbishop's two reasons for leading the rebels are 'brother general' and 'brother born'. First, a general reason: on behalf of all the people of England ('the commonwealth'). Second, a particular personal reason: his brother's death. He refers to an earlier event when Bullingbrook, later to become Henry IV, executed Lord Scroop at Bristol, without allowing him even to receive the last sacrament from a priest ('unhouseled').

Mowbray's reason for rebellion is dramatised in *Richard II*. At the start of that play, Mowbray's father (the Duke of Norfolk) quarrels with Bullingbrook, and the two meet at Coventry in a tournament. They were ready to fight, standing in their saddles ('roused in their seats'), their lances at the ready, their helmet face-guards closed ('beavers down'). But King Richard threw down his staff of office ('warder') to stop the fight. That act brought about England's misfortunes, because Bullingbrook deposed Richard, became king and caused many deaths (lines 127–9).

Find a copy of *Richard II* and remind yourself of Shakespeare's dramatisation of the above events in Act 1 Scene 3 (the tournament at Coventry and the banishment of Mowbray), and Act 3 Scene 2, lines 141–2 where the execution of Scroop (the Earl of Wiltshire) is reported.

## 2 'Necessities'

Don't blame King Henry, blame the necessities of the times, says Westmoreland (lines 103–6). For information on 'necessities' (facts, politics, practicalities), see page 194.

---

**gallèd** hurt
**suborned to grate on** bribed to harass
**commotion's bitter edge** the swords of rebels
**the days before** past times

**unequal hand** unfair force
**Construe** interpret
**signories** estates and titles
**force perforce** willy nilly, by force
**stayed** stopped, held back

WESTMORELAND  Whenever yet was your appeal denied?
            Wherein have you been gallèd by the king?
            What peer hath been suborned to grate on you,                90
            That you should seal this lawless bloody book
            Of forged rebellion with a seal divine,
            And consecrate commotion's bitter edge?
ARCHBISHOP  My brother general: the commonwealth.
            To brother born unhouseled cruelty                            95
            I make my quarrel in particular.
WESTMORELAND  There is no need of any such redress,
            Or, if there were, it not belongs to you.
MOWBRAY  Why not to him in part, and to us all
            That feel the bruises of the days before,                     100
            And suffer the condition of these times
            To lay a heavy and unequal hand
            Upon our honours.
WESTMORELAND            O my good Lord Mowbray,
            Construe the times to their necessities,
            And you shall say indeed it is the time                       105
            And not the king that doth you injuries.
            Yet for your part it not appears to me
            Either from the king or in the present time
            That you should have an inch of any ground
            To build a grief on. Were you not restored                    110
            To all the Duke of Norfolk's signories,
            Your noble and right well-remembered father's?
MOWBRAY  What thing, in honour, had my father lost
            That need to be revived and breathed in me?
            The king that loved him, as the state stood then,            115
            Was force perforce compelled to banish him,
            And then that Henry Bullingbrook and he
            Being mounted and both rousèd in their seats,
            Their neighing coursers daring of the spur,
            Their armèd staves in charge, their beavers down,            120
            Their eyes of fire sparkling through sights of steel,
            And the loud trumpet blowing them together,
            Then, then, when there was nothing could have stayed
            My father from the breast of Bullingbrook,
            O, when the king did throw his warder down,                  125
            His own life hung upon the staff he threw.

*Westmoreland rejects Mowbray's claim, saying that the people loved Bullingbrook. He offers peace talks to the rebels. Mowbray is suspicious, but Hastings seems willing to negotiate with Prince John.*

## 1 'All the country'

Westmoreland is unconvinced by Mowbray's story that Bullingbrook (King Henry) has caused all the bloodshed and troubles in England. He argues that even if Mowbray's father had killed Bullingbrook (and the outcome of the tournament was uncertain), he would not have got out of Coventry alive ('ne'er had borne it out'), because all the people of England loved Bullingbrook, and would have risen against Mowbray.

Politicians today and all through the ages claim that they have the people on their side and that they act in the best interests of the people. Both the Archbishop (line 94) and Westmoreland make that claim. As you read on, keep thinking about whether such claims are genuine, or whether both the rebels and the king are really fighting to maintain their power and control over the ordinary people of England.

## 2 Using repetition for effect

Westmoreland is emphatic in claiming that his side's forces are stronger than the rebels. Speak his lines 149–58, emphasising each use of 'our'.

## 3 'A rotten case' (in pairs)

Westmoreland taunts Mowbray with a proverb at line 161: just as a badly made box won't stand being knocked about ('handling'), so a poor argument can't stand up to questioning. Use Activity 3 on page 42 to talk together about why this proverb is no longer in common use.

---

**indictment** legal accusation
**dint** force
**Earl of Hereford** Bullingbrook (Henry IV)
**mere digression** a petty diversion
**set off** forgotten, put aside
**policy** cunning, statecraft

**overween** presume
**a ken** sight
**names** numbers, knights
**parley** peace talks
**commission** authority
**In very ample virtue of** acting for

Then threw he down himself and all their lives
That by indictment and by dint of sword
Have since miscarried under Bullingbrook.
WESTMORELAND  You speak, Lord Mowbray, now you know not
        what.                                              130
The Earl of Hereford was reputed then
In England the most valiant gentleman.
Who knows on whom fortune would then have smiled?
But if your father had been victor there,
He ne'er had borne it out at Coventry,                     135
For all the country, in a general voice,
Cried hate upon him, and all their prayers and love
Were set on Hereford, whom they doted on,
And blessed and graced indeed more than the king.
But this is mere digression from my purpose.               140
Here come I from our princely general
To know your griefs, to tell you from his grace
That he will give you audience; and wherein
It shall appear that your demands are just,
You shall enjoy them, everything set off                   145
That might so much as think you enemies.
MOWBRAY  But he hath forced us to compel this offer,
And it proceeds from policy, not love.
WESTMORELAND  Mowbray, you overween to take it so:
This offer comes from mercy, not from fear,                150
For lo, within a ken our army lies,
Upon mine honour, all too confident
To give admittance to a thought of fear.
Our battle is more full of names than yours,
Our men more perfect in the use of arms,                   155
Our armour all as strong, our cause the best;
Then reason will our hearts should be as good.
Say you not then our offer is compelled.
MOWBRAY  Well, by my will we shall admit no parley.
WESTMORELAND  That argues but the shame of your offence:   160
A rotten case abides no handling.
HASTINGS  Hath the Prince John a full commission,
In very ample virtue of his father,
To hear and absolutely to determine
Of what conditions we shall stand upon?                    165

*The Archbishop gives Westmoreland a schedule of the rebels' grievances to take to Prince John. If they are resolved, the rebellion will end. Mowbray is uneasy, but Hastings expresses optimism.*

## 1 The schedule

Write out the schedule that the Archbishop hands to Westmoreland. List the grievances that the rebels want redressed (see pages 1, 112 and 191).

## 2 Imagery: help the audience (in pairs)

a Line 176: 'our aweful banks'. The Archbishop promises that if the rebels' demands are met, and pardon offered, the rebels will 'come within our aweful banks again'. Work out the image he probably has in mind, remembering that by 'awe' he means 'paying respect that is due'.

The audience are likely to hear the word as 'awful'. How can the actor playing the Archbishop help the audience to grasp his meaning?

b Lines 194–6: 'We shall be winnowed'. Mowbray does not trust Prince John or Westmoreland, but Hastings and the Archbishop overrule him. Mowbray suspects that even if peace is obtained, the rebels will be regarded in low esteem ('valuation') by King Henry. He will be reminded of their rebellion by every trivial incident.

Mowbray uses a vivid image to express the consequence. Wheat was 'winnowed' (tossed into the air), to separate the corn from the chaff (the useless husks which were blown away by the wind). But King Henry's winnowing will create such a rough wind that everyone will suffer: the rebels will be swept away with any trivial offenders.

Invent some 'business' for Mowbray to help the audience with the image.

---

| | |
|---|---|
| **muse** am surprised | **large terms** all-encompassing |
| **several** individual | demands |
| **ensinewed to** joined together in | **valuation** esteem |
| **Acquitted** pardoned | **nice and wanton** petty and |
| **substantial form** genuine order | frivolous |
| **present execution** immediate | **taste** remind |
| carrying out | **partition** difference, separation |

WESTMORELAND  That is intended in the general's name.
    I muse you make so slight a question.
ARCHBISHOP  Then take, my Lord of Westmoreland, this
    schedule,
    For this contains our general grievances.
    Each several article herein redressed,                170
    All members of our cause, both here and hence,
    That are ensinewed to this action,
    Acquitted by a true substantial form
    And present execution of our wills,
    To us and our purposes confined                 175
    We come within our aweful banks again
    And knit our powers to the arm of peace.
WESTMORELAND  This will I show the general. Please you, lords,
    In sight of both our battles we may meet
    At either end in peace – which God so frame –       180
    Or to the place of difference call the swords
    Which must decide it.
ARCHBISHOP                 My lord, we will do so.

*Exit Westmoreland*

MOWBRAY  There is a thing within my bosom tells me
    That no conditions of our peace can stand.
HASTINGS  Fear you not, that if we can make our peace     185
    Upon such large terms, and so absolute,
    As our conditions shall consist upon,
    Our peace shall stand as firm as rocky mountains.
MOWBRAY  Yea, but our valuation shall be such
    That every slight and false-derivèd cause,        190
    Yea, every idle, nice and wanton reason,
    Shall to the king taste of this action,
    That, were our royal faiths martyrs in love,
    We shall be winnowed with so rough a wind
    That even our corn shall seem as light as chaff,     195
    And good from bad find no partition.

*The Archbishop claims that King Henry will not punish the rebels, for fear of making more enemies. Hastings adds that the king's army is weakened by fighting Hotspur and other rebels.*

## 1 Reasons (in pairs)

The Archbishop offers two major reasons why King Henry will not punish the rebels (first, vengeance; second, friends and foes). Hastings adds a third reason (weakness). Identify the lines that state all three reasons, and express them in your own language.

## 2 Imagery creates meaning (in pairs)

Suggest how each of the following images helps to create the speaker's meaning:

lines 201–4 'tables' – notebooks

lines 205–9 'weed'

lines 215–17 'rods' – weapons, soldiers

## 3 Personal experience?

Imagine someone says to you 'Shakespeare used his own personal experience as he wrote lines 210–14'. What do you reply?

## 4 Cheering themselves up? (in pairs)

Do the Archbishop and Hastings really believe what they say? Or do they, like Mowbray, feel uneasy about what King Henry will really do?

Step into role as the characters and try two very different versions of how to deliver their lines opposite. In the first, the two men are full of confidence, believing absolutely what they say. Make your second version one in which they hope what they say is true, but do not really believe it.

How does Mowbray, the doubter, speak 'Be it so' (line 223)?

---

dainty ... picking  trivial
heirs of life  survivors
telltale  reminder
history  recall
weed this land  kill his enemies
offer strokes  raise his fist

resolved correction  intended punishment
late offenders  previous rebels
atonement  reconciliation
just distance  half way

ARCHBISHOP  No, no, my lord, note this: the king is weary
        Of dainty and such picking grievances,
        For he hath found to end one doubt by death
        Revives two greater in the heirs of life,        200
        And therefore will he wipe his tables clean
        And keep no telltale to his memory
        That may repeat and history his loss
        To new remembrance; for full well he knows
        He cannot so precisely weed this land        205
        As his misdoubts present occasion:
        His foes are so enrooted with his friends
        That, plucking to unfix the enemy,
        He doth unfasten so and shake a friend.
        So that this land, like an offensive wife        210
        That hath enraged him on to offer strokes,
        As he is striking, holds his infant up
        And hangs resolved correction in the arm
        That was upreared to execution.
HASTINGS  Besides, the king hath wasted all his rods        215
        On late offenders, that he now doth lack
        The very instruments of chastisement,
        So that his power, like a fangless lion,
        May offer, but not hold.
ARCHBISHOP                'Tis very true;
        And therefore be assured, my good lord marshal,        220
        If we do now make our atonement well,
        Our peace will, like a broken limb reunited,
        Grow stronger for the breaking.
MOWBRAY                Be it so.
        Here is returned my Lord of Westmoreland.

        *Enter* WESTMORELAND

WESTMORELAND  The prince is here at hand. Pleaseth your lord-
        ship        225
        To meet his grace just distance 'tween our armies.
MOWBRAY  Your grace of York, in God's name then set forward.
ARCHBISHOP  [To *Mowbray*] Before, and greet his grace. – My lord, we
        come.

*Prince John rebukes the Archbishop for turning from religion to warfare.*
*He says that the Archbishop is the mediator between God and men, but*
*now challenges God's deputy, the king.*

## 1 Criticising the Archbishop (in small groups)

Explore ways of speaking John's lines to convey John's criticism that a
man of God should be preaching the gospel, and supporting the king,
not leading an armed rebellion. The following points can help you:

a 'Cousin Mowbray'. Mowbray is not related to John. It was
common practice among nobles at the time to use 'cousin' or 'coz'
as a form of address.

b John uses contrasts of good and bad behaviour throughout his
speech. Try to bring out those contrasts in your delivery.
Sometimes the contrasts run over several lines (as in lines 232–7).
Other contrasts are in a single line or phrase, as in 'word to sword
(Bible to battle), and life to death' (line 238).

c 'His substitute' (line 256). Medieval and Tudor monarchs knew
that they could more easily keep control if their subjects believed
in the Divine Right of Kings: that the king was God's deputy on
earth. To rebel against the king was to rebel against God (see page
191).

## 2 'An iron man'

Use the clues in lines 45 and 236 to design the Archbishop's costume
('an iron man' = in armour, merciless).

---

**flock** congregation
**exposition** sermon
**set abroach** open up
**speaker in His parliament**
  intermediary between God and man
**opener and intelligencer**
  interpreter and messenger

**dull workings** unclear minds
**Imply** employ
**false favourite** deceitful courtier
**ta'en up** enlisted
**upswarmed** clustered them like a
  swarm of bees

*Enter Prince* JOHN [*of Lancaster*] *and his army*

JOHN You are well encountered here, my cousin Mowbray;
      Good day to you, gentle Lord Archbishop,      230
      And so to you, Lord Hastings, and to all.
      My Lord of York, it better showed with you
      When that your flock, assembled by the bell,
      Encircled you to hear with reverence
      Your exposition on the holy text,      235
      Than now to see you here an iron man talking,
      Cheering a rout of rebels with your drum,
      Turning the word to sword, and life to death.
      That man that sits within a monarch's heart
      And ripens in the sunshine of his favour,      240
      Would he abuse the countenance of the king?
      Alack, what mischiefs might he set abroach
      In shadow of such greatness! With you, Lord Bishop,
      It is even so. Who hath not heard it spoken
      How deep you were within the books of God?      245
      To us the speaker in His parliament,
      To us th'imagined voice of God himself,
      The very opener and intelligencer
      Between the grace, the sanctities of heaven
      And our dull workings. O, who shall believe      250
      But you misuse the reverence of your place,
      Imply the countenance and grace of heaven
      As a false favourite doth his prince's name
      In deeds dishonourable? You have ta'en up,
      Under the counterfeited zeal of God,      255
      The subjects of His substitute, my father,
      And both against the peace of heaven and him
      Have here upswarmed them.

*The Archbishop protests that the rebellion is not against the king, but against abuses of social order. If those abuses are resolved, the rebels will obey the king. Prince John promises redress of all the grievances.*

Hastings, the Archbishop, Mowbray. Are the rebels surprised by the speed with which Prince John accepts their demands? Suggest how each man might react physically to John's line 282.

## 1 Prince John: is he sincere? (in pairs)

Speak all Prince John's lines opposite to convey how his tone changes from his rebuke to Hastings to his offer of peace. Emphasise all his words of trust: 'swear', 'honour', 'soul', 'friendly', 'embrace', 'love and amity'. Then say whether you (like the Archbishop) trust John's word.

**monstrous form** unnatural shape
(armed rebellion)
**parcels** details
**Hydra** many-headed monster
which grew two heads for every
one cut off
**fall down** are defeated

**supplies** reinforcements
**generation** children
**sound the bottom of the after-
times** plumb the depths of the
future
**articles** conditions
**Wrested** twisted

ARCHBISHOP                    Good my Lord of Lancaster,
        I am not here against your father's peace,
        But, as I told my Lord of Westmoreland,                    260
        The time misordered doth, in common sense,
        Crowd us and crush us to this monstrous form
        To hold our safety up. I sent your grace
        The parcels and particulars of our grief,
        The which hath been with scorn shoved from the court,      265
        Whereon this Hydra son of war is born,
        Whose dangerous eyes may well be charmed asleep
        With grant of our most just and right desires,
        And true obedience, of this madness cured,
        Stoop tamely to the foot of majesty.                       270
MOWBRAY  If not, we ready are to try our fortunes
        To the last man.
HASTINGS                  And though we here fall down
        We have supplies to second our attempt;
        If they miscarry, theirs shall second them,
        And so success of mischief shall be born,                  275
        And heir from heir shall hold his quarrel up
        Whiles England shall have generation.
JOHN  You are too shallow, Hastings, much too shallow
        To sound the bottom of the after-times.
WESTMORELAND  Pleaseth your grace to answer them directly        280
        How far forth you do like their articles.
JOHN  I like them all, and do allow them well,
        And swear here by the honour of my blood,
        My father's purposes have been mistook,
        And some about him have too lavishly                       285
        Wrested his meaning and authority.
        My lord, these griefs shall be with speed redressed,
        Upon my soul they shall. If this may please you,
        Discharge your powers unto their several counties
        As we will ours; and here, between the armies,             290
        Let's drink together, friendly, and embrace,
        That all their eyes may bear those tokens home
        Of our restorèd love and amity.
ARCHBISHOP  I take your princely word for these redresses.

*Orders are given to dismiss the rebel army. Prince John and the rebels drink together, but Mowbray has ominous fears. John proposes that both armies march past for inspection.*

## 1 Mowbray's fears, the Archbishop's optimism

Mowbray feels uneasy about John's quick acceptance of all the rebels' demands, and the promise of peace. The Archbishop puts an optimistic interpretation on Mowbray's fears. His line 309 echoes Romeo's words as he prepares to take his own life:

'How oft when men are at the point of death
Have they been merry'
(*Romeo and Juliet*, Act 5 Scene 3, lines 88–9)

The Archbishop adds another proverb, saying that sadness precedes something pleasant ('heaviness foreruns the good event'). Mowbray is not comforted, and hearing the Archbishop say that he feels extremely cheerful ('passing light') reminds him of his own rule that cheerfulness precedes disaster.

The contrasting attitudes of Mowbray and the Archbishop are further shown in their reponse to hearing the rebel soldiers' cheers (lines 316–19).

At this moment in the play which of the two men seems to you to have a firmer understanding of the reality of what is happening?

## 2 The march past (in pairs)

Why do the two leaders think that a march past by both armies is a good idea? Step into role as the Archbishop and Prince John and state your reasons for ordering a march past.

---

**Hie thee** hurry
**pledge** drink to
**bestowed** taken, given (all
  Westmoreland's words are ironical)
**heaviness** sadness

**rendered** proclaimed
**trains** armies
**peruse** inspect
**coped withal** fought with

JOHN  I give it you and will maintain my word,                              295
         And thereupon I drink unto your grace.
HASTINGS  Go, captain, and deliver to the army
         This news of peace. Let them have pay, and part,
         I know it will well please them. Hie thee, captain.

                                              *Exit [Captain]*

ARCHBISHOP  To you, my noble Lord of Westmoreland.              300
WESTMORELAND  I pledge your grace; and if you knew what pains
         I have bestowed to breed this present peace
         You would drink freely. But my love to ye
         Shall show itself more openly hereafter.
ARCHBISHOP  I do not doubt you.
WESTMORELAND                   I am glad of it.                       305
         Health to my lord and gentle cousin Mowbray.
MOWBRAY  You wish me health in very happy season,
         For I am on the sudden something ill.
ARCHBISHOP  Against ill chances men are ever merry,
         But heaviness foreruns the good event.               310
WESTMORELAND  Therefore be merry, coz, since sudden
                  sorrow
         Serves to say thus: some good thing comes tomorrow.
ARCHBISHOP  Believe me, I am passing light in spirit.
MOWBRAY  So much the worse, if your own rule be true.

                       *Shout [within]*

JOHN  The word of peace is rendered. Hark how they shout!      315
MOWBRAY  This had been cheerful after victory.
ARCHBISHOP  A peace is of the nature of a conquest,
         For then both parties nobly are subdued
         And neither party loser.
JOHN                        Go, my lord,
         And let our army be dischargèd too.                   320

                               *Exit [Westmoreland]*

         And, good my lord, so please you, let our trains
         March by us, that we may peruse the men
         We should have coped withal.
ARCHBISHOP                    Go, good Lord Hastings,
         And, ere they be dismissed, let them march by.

                                        *Exit [Hastings]*

*Prince John's army awaits his orders. Hastings reports that the rebel army has dispersed. The rebels are arrested and sentenced to death. John justifies his action saying it is honourable and Christian.*

## 1 Victory by deceit (in small groups)

Lines 282–351 show the rebels falling into the trap set by Prince John and Westmoreland. Choose one or more of the following:

a Take parts and enact the lines. Try especially to bring out the 'double speak' of Westmoreland and John. Their words seem friendly, but they contain a deeper meaning.

b Westmoreland and John have obviously plotted their deception carefully. Take parts and improvise their meeting in which they work out their plan.

c All armies keep a war diary. It is written up daily and tells what happened on that day. Step into Westmoreland's shoes and write up his account of the events in Gaultree Forest.

d Has John behaved with honour? Speak all the words and phrases he uses to reassure the rebels of his honourable intentions.

e Does John behave with 'a most Christian care' (line 343)? At the time, it was the official doctrine of the church that faith need not be kept with heretics. A heretic was defined as a non-believer, and rebels were seen as heretics. Promises made to them had no legal or moral force. Give your own view of that doctrine, and whether it applies today. For example, should governments keep promises made during negotiations with terrorists?

f Invent a gesture or action each character might use as they leave the stage at line 351.

---

**lie tonight together** sleep in peace
**unyoked** set free
**attach** arrest
**assembly** rebel army
**pawned** pledged

**Meet for** appropriate to
**Fondly** ill-advisedly
**stray** stragglers
*Alarum. Excursions* trumpet calls
  and combats

JOHN  I trust, lords, we shall lie tonight together.                    325

*Enter* WESTMORELAND

Now, cousin, wherefore stands our army still?
WESTMORELAND  The leaders, having charge from you to stand,
Will not go off until they hear you speak.
JOHN  They know their duties.

*Enter* HASTINGS

HASTINGS  My lord, our army is dispersed already.                    330
Like youthful steers unyoked they take their courses
East, West, North, South, or like a school broke up,
Each hurries toward his home and sporting-place.
WESTMORELAND  Good tidings, my Lord Hastings, for the which
I do arrest thee, traitor, of high treason –                    335
And you, Lord Archbishop, and you, Lord Mowbray,
Of capital treason I attach you both.
MOWBRAY  Is this proceeding just and honourable?
WESTMORELAND  Is your assembly so?
ARCHBISHOP  Will you thus break your faith?
JOHN                              I pawned thee none.                    340
I promised you redress of these same grievances
Whereof you did complain, which by mine honour
I will perform with a most Christian care.
But for you rebels, look to taste the due
Meet for rebellion.                    345
Most shallowly did you these arms commence,
Fondly brought here, and foolishly sent hence.
Strike up our drums, pursue the scattered stray:
God, and not we, hath safely fought today.
Some guard these traitors to the block of death,                    350
Treason's true bed and yielder up of breath.

*Exeunt*

*Alarum. Excursions. Enter* FALSTAFF *and Sir John* COLEVILE

*Colevile surrenders to Falstaff who reflects that his size tells everyone who he is. Prince John chides Falstaff for lateness, but Falstaff claims he has ridden post-haste and has captured Colevile. John is unimpressed.*

## 1 Comedy after treachery (in groups of three)

Lines 352–408 present a comic episode. It reflects a similar scene in *Part 1* in which Falstaff claims to have killed Hotspur. Take parts as Falstaff, John and Colevile (one of the stragglers who Prince John ordered to be pursued). Act out the lines, using the suggestions below and on page 130.

- How do Falstaff and Colevile enter? Do they actually fight, or circle each other, both afraid to strike?
- Is Colevile really afraid of Falstaff? Is Falstaff brave, or just bragging in the hope that Colevile will surrender without a fight?
- Just how does Colevile surrender to Falstaff?
- What gestures might Falstaff make in lines 365–8 when he tells that his huge belly always proclaims who he is, and that he would be much more active if only it were a normal size?

## 2 Who? Me?

Falstaff uses one of his typical tricks as he defends himself against John's accusation of late arrival ('tardy tricks'). Speak his lines 376–85 with an air of injured innocence ('foundered nine score and odd posts' means lamed more than 180 horses).

Think about whether he changes his tone towards the end when he compares himself with Julius Caesar ('the hook-nosed fellow of Rome') who said 'I came, I saw, I conquered'.

---

| | |
|---|---|
| **condition** rank | **womb** belly |
| **degree** status | *Retreat* trumpet call |
| **yield** surrender | **heat** battle |
| **lovers** mourners | **powers** troops |
| **do observance** pay homage, respect | **rebuke and check** criticism |
| **indifferency** ordinary size | **expedition** speed |

FALSTAFF  What's your name, sir, of what condition are you, and of what
place?

COLEVILE  I am a knight, sir, and my name is Colevile of the Dale.

FALSTAFF  Well then, Colevile is your name, a knight is your degree, and   355
your place the dale. Colevile shall be still your name, a traitor your
degree, and the dungeon your place, a place deep enough; so shall
you be still Colevile of the Dale.

COLEVILE  Are not you Sir John Falstaff?

FALSTAFF  As good a man as he, sir, whoe'er I am. Do ye yield, sir, or shall   360
I sweat for you? If I do sweat, they are the drops of thy lovers, and
they weep for thy death; therefore rouse up fear and trembling, and
do observance to my mercy.

COLEVILE  I think you are Sir John Falstaff, and in that thought yield me.

FALSTAFF  I have a whole school of tongues in this belly of mine, and not   365
a tongue of them all speaks any other word but my name. And I had
but a belly of any indifferency, I were simply the most active fellow
in Europe. My womb, my womb, my womb undoes me. – Here
comes our general.

*Retreat. Enter Prince* JOHN, WESTMORELAND *and the rest*

JOHN  The heat is past, follow no further now,   370
Call in the powers, good cousin Westmoreland.

[*Exit Westmoreland*]

Now, Falstaff, where have you been all this while?
When everything is ended, then you come:
These tardy tricks of yours will, on my life,
One time or other break some gallows' back.   375

FALSTAFF  I would be sorry, my lord, but it should be thus. I never knew
yet but rebuke and check was the reward of valour. Do you think me
a swallow, an arrow, or a bullet? Have I, in my poor and old motion,
the expedition of thought? I have speeded hither with the very
extremest inch of possibility, I have foundered nine score and odd   380
posts; and here, travel-tainted as I am, have in my pure and
immaculate valour taken Sir John Colevile of the Dale, a most
furious knight and valorous enemy. But what of that? He saw me
and yielded, that I may justly say, with the hook-nosed fellow of
Rome, 'There, cousin, I came, saw, and overcame.'   385

JOHN  It was more of his courtesy than your deserving.

*Falstaff asks that his bravery be honoured – or else! Prince John orders the execution of Colevile and the other rebels. He reports that King Henry is sick. Falstaff is granted leave to travel through Gloucestershire.*

## 1 'A particular ballad'

Falstaff threatens that if he does not receive the praise and reward due to him ('let it be booked'), he will write 'a particular (all about me) ballad', illustrated with a drawing of himself and Colevile.

Write and illustrate Falstaff's ballad. Remember that he says that Prince John and the others will appear in it, portrayed as grossly inferior to his own bravery ('gilt twopences' were twopenny coins painted gold by counterfeiters to look like higher-value coins).

## 2 Funny? (in pairs)

Does Prince John have a sense of humour? Speak John's exchange with Falstaff at lines 394–9, then say what you think of it.

## 3 'A famous rebel'

Colevile claims that he urged the rebels to fight, but the whole Colevile episode is Shakespeare's invention. The only record of Colevile is in Holinshed (see page 202). There, he is simply reported as being executed at Durham by King Henry as the king's army marched North.

Did Shakespeare just like the sound of Colevile's name, or did he have specific dramatic purposes in mind for the episode? When you have read to the end of the scene, make one or two suggestions about the dramatic function of lines 352–413.

---

**booked** recorded
**cinders of the element** stars in the night sky
**let desert mount** give me high praise
**won them dearer** suffered more casualties

**gratis** freely
**stayed** halted
**present execution** immediate death
**sober** proper
**stand my good lord** sponsor me
**condition** rank as commander-in-chief

FALSTAFF I know not: here he is, and here I yield him, and I beseech your
grace let it be booked with the rest of this day's deeds, or, by the Lord, I
will have it in a particular ballad else, with mine own picture on the top
on't, Colevile kissing my foot. To the which course if I be enforced, if      390
you do not all show like gilt twopences to me and I in the clear sky of
Fame o'ershine you as much as the full moon doth the cinders of the
element (which show like pins' heads to her), believe not the word of
the noble. Therefore let me have right, and let desert mount.

JOHN Thine's too heavy to mount.                                              395

FALSTAFF Let it shine then.

JOHN Thine's too thick to shine.

FALSTAFF Let it do something, my good lord, that may do me good, and
call it what you will.

JOHN Is thy name Colevile?                                                    400

COLEVILE It is, my lord.

JOHN A famous rebel art thou, Colevile.

FALSTAFF And a famous true subject took him.

COLEVILE I am, my lord, but as my betters are
          That led me hither. Had they been ruled by me,                     405
          You should have won them dearer than you have.

FALSTAFF I know not how they sold themselves, but thou like a kind
fellow gavest thyself away gratis, and I thank thee for thee.

*Enter* WESTMORELAND

JOHN Now, have you left pursuit?

WESTMORELAND Retreat is made, and execution stayed.                          410

JOHN Send Colevile with his confederates
     To York, to present execution.
     Blunt, lead him hence and see you guard him sure.

                         *Exit [Blunt] with Colevile*

     And now dispatch we toward the court, my lords,
     I hear the king my father is sore sick.                                  415
     Our news shall go before us to his majesty,
     Which, cousin, you shall bear to comfort him,
     And we with sober speed will follow you.

FALSTAFF My lord, I beseech you give me leave to go through
Gloucestershire, and when you come to court, stand my good lord              420
in your good report.

JOHN Fare you well, Falstaff. I, in my condition,
     Shall better speak of you than you deserve.

                              *Exeunt all but Falstaff*

*Falstaff reflects that Prince John's cold personality comes from not drinking wine. He praises the results of drinking sack, claiming it sharpens wit and increases bravery. He resolves to exploit Justice Shallow.*

Falstaff reflects that 'sherris-sack' (a strong white wine from Jerez in Spain) makes a man witty and courageous. Speak Falstaff's soliloquy, then invent a response to it, in the same style, as a member of Alcoholics Anonymous.

## 1 Sealing wax

Falstaff's final thoughts turn to how he might acquire some of Justice Shallow's wealth. He thinks of Shallow as a piece of sealing wax between his finger and thumb, which he is softening ('tempering') to mould to any shape he pleases. Speak Falstaff's final four lines with appropriate expression and gestures.

**any proof** be a real man
**get wenches** father girls
**inflammation** the effect of drink
**crudy** curdled, thick
**environ** surround
**forgetive** creative (as in a forge)
**pusillanimity** faint-heartedness

**extremes** extremities, limbs
**vital commoners and inland**
 **petty spirits** every part of the body
**muster me** rally
**retinue** army
**thin potations** weak drink

FALSTAFF  I would you had the wit: 'twere better than your dukedom. Good faith, this same young sober-blooded boy doth not love me, nor a man cannot make him laugh. But that's no marvel, he drinks no wine. There's never none of these demure boys come to any proof, for thin drink doth so overcool their blood, and making many fish meals, that they fall into a kind of male green-sickness, and then when they marry they get wenches. They are generally fools and cowards – which some of us should be too, but for inflammation. A good sherris-sack hath a twofold operation in it: it ascends me into the brain, dries me there all the foolish and dull and crudy vapours which environ it, makes it apprehensive, quick, forgetive, full of nimble, fiery and delectable shapes, which delivered o'er to the voice, the tongue, which is the birth, becomes excellent wit. The second property of your excellent sherris is the warming of the blood, which before, cold and settled, left the liver white and pale, which is the badge of pusillanimity and cowardice; but the sherris warms it and makes it course from the inwards to the parts' extremes: it illumineth the face which, as a beacon, gives warning to all the rest of this little kingdom – man – to arm; and then the vital commoners and inland petty spirits muster me all to their captain, the heart, who, great and puffed up with this retinue, doth any deed of courage: and this valour comes of sherris. So that skill in the weapon is nothing without sack, for that sets it a-work; and learning a mere hoard of gold kept by a devil, till sack commences it and sets it in act and use. Hereof comes it that Prince Harry is valiant, for the cold blood he did naturally inherit of his father he hath, like lean, sterile and bare land, manured, husbanded and tilled, with excellent endeavour of drinking good and good store of fertile sherris, that he is become very hot and valiant. If I had a thousand sons, the first human principle I would teach them should be to forswear thin potations, and to addict themselves to sack.

*Enter* BARDOLPH

How now, Bardolph?

BARDOLPH  The army is dischargèd all and gone.

FALSTAFF  Let them go. I'll through Gloucestershire, and there will I visit Master Robert Shallow, esquire. I have him already tempering between my finger and my thumb, and shortly will I seal with him. Come away.

*Exeunt*

*King Henry proposes a crusade to the Holy Land. The army and navy*
*are ready, but the king's health and the rebellion cause delay.*
*Henry asks the whereabouts of Hal.*

## 1 The Jerusalem Chamber

At the end of Act 3 Scene 1, and in two earlier plays (*Richard II* and
*Henry IV Part 1*), Henry proposed a crusade to the Holy Land to
recapture Jerusalem for Christianity. He believed that such a
crusade would help expiate his sin for overthrowing the rightful king,
Richard II. Now Henry again declares his intention of leading a
crusade (lines 3–7).

Design the set for this scene. The Jerusalem Chamber was a room in
Westminster Abbey. It was so called because of inscriptions around
the fireplace mentioning Jerusalem.

## 2 Does Gloucester know? (in pairs)

Gloucester is Henry's youngest son. He tells his sick father that he does
not know who Hal's companions are (line 15). Is he telling the truth?
Explore different ways and motives for Gloucester to deliver his reply
for each of the following:

• He really does not know.

• He suspects Hal is with Poins and others from the tavern.

• He knows Hal is with Poins and the others.

Suggest several reasons why Henry wants to know Hal's whereabouts.

---

**debate** civil war
**higher fields** more exalted
  battlefields
**sanctified** blessed as holy
**addressed** prepared

**power** army
**substitutes** deputies
**well invested** granted full powers
**pause us** delay
**afoot** active
**yoke** restraint

# ACT 4   SCENE 2
## The Jerusalem Chamber in Westminster Abbey


*Enter the* KING, *carried in a chair,* WARWICK,
*Thomas Duke of* CLARENCE, *Humphrey Duke of* GLOUCESTER,
*and Attendants*

KING  Now lords, if God doth give successful end
       To this debate that bleedeth at our doors,
       We will our youth lead on to higher fields,
       And draw no swords but what are sanctified:
       Our navy is addressed, our power collected,        5
       Our substitutes in absence well invested,
       And everything lies level to our wish;
       Only we want a little personal strength,
       And pause us till these rebels now afoot
       Come underneath the yoke of government.        10
WARWICK  Both which we doubt not but your majesty
       Shall soon enjoy.
KING                  Humphrey my son of Gloucester,
       Where is the prince your brother?
GLOUCESTER  I think he's gone to hunt, my lord, at
       Windsor.
KING  And how accompanied?
GLOUCESTER              I do not know, my lord.        15
KING  Is not his brother Thomas of Clarence with him?
GLOUCESTER No, my good lord, he is in presence here.
CLARENCE  What would my lord and father?

> *Henry advises Clarence to make firm friends with Hal, whose temperament is changeable but noble. Such friendship will strengthen the royal family. Henry fears the influence of the tavern on Hal.*

## 1 Giving advice (in small groups)

Henry is a sick man, near to death. He wants to ensure that his sons do not fight each other after his death. He advises Clarence to cement his friendship with Hal, the future King Henry V, and to choose his time very carefully when he wants to criticise him. In that way, future strife can be avoided.

Take turns to speak Henry's lines as you think a gravely-ill king and father would.

Think about each of the following:

a What gestures and actions might Henry perform to accompany and emphasise what he says?

b What impression of Hal's character is given in lines 30–5? Does it match your own impression of Hal?

c Express the following images in your own words, then give one or two reasons for whether or not you find each image appropriate to the meaning you think Henry wishes to convey:
'a tear for pity' (line 31)
'a hand/Open as day' (lines 31–2)
'flint' (line 33)
'As humorous as winter … spring of day' (lines 34–5)
a stranded whale (lines 39–41)
a golden-hooped barrel (lines 43–8)
weeds growing on fertile ground (line 54).

d What does Clarence do throughout Henry's speech?

---

**offices** duties
**mediation** reconciliation
**omit** neglect
**observed** respected, humoured
**meting** sharing out
**humorous** capricious, moody
**flaws congealèd … day** hail storms

**Confound … working** destroy themselves with overexertion
**venom of suggestion** poison of suspicion
**aconitum** wolfsbane, a poisonous plant
**fattest** most fertile

KING   Nothing but well to thee, Thomas of Clarence.
       How chance thou art not with the prince thy brother?    20
       He loves thee, and thou dost neglect him, Thomas.
       Thou hast a better place in his affection
       Than all thy brothers; cherish it, my boy,
       And noble offices thou mayst effect
       Of mediation, after I am dead,    25
       Between his greatness and thy other brethren.
       Therefore omit him not, blunt not his love,
       Nor lose the good advantage of his grace
       By seeming cold or careless of his will,
       For he is gracious if he be observed,    30
       He hath a tear for pity, and a hand
       Open as day for meting charity;
       Yet notwithstanding, being incensed, he is flint,
       As humorous as winter, and as sudden
       As flaws congealèd in the spring of day.    35
       His temper therefore must be well observed;
       Chide him for faults, and do it reverently,
       When you perceive his blood inclined to mirth;
       But, being moody, give him time and scope,
       Till that his passions, like a whale on ground,    40
       Confound themselves with working. Learn this, Thomas,
       And thou shalt prove a shelter to thy friends,
       A hoop of gold to bind thy brothers in,
       That the united vessel of their blood,
       Mingled with venom of suggestion,    45
       As force perforce the age will pour it in,
       Shall never leak, though it do work as strong
       As aconitum, or rash gunpowder.
CLARENCE   I shall observe him with all care and love.
KING   Why art thou not at Windsor with him, Thomas?    50
CLARENCE   He is not there today, he dines in London.
KING   And how accompanied?
CLARENCE   With Poins and other his continual followers.
KING   Most subject is the fattest soil to weeds,
       And he, the noble image of my youth,    55
       Is overspread with them, therefore my grief
       Stretches itself beyond the hour of death.

*Henry fears Hal will be unable to resist corruption when he becomes king. Warwick says that Hal learns from his tavern acquaintances, but will reject them. Henry doubts it. News of peace arrives.*

## 1 Who is right?

Henry thinks that after his death, Hal will continue his old self-centred way of life, ruled by his baser passions. Once he has the means to indulge his desires, Hal will be unwilling to face dangers and hostile attacks ('fronting peril and opposed decay') on his own morality or on England.

Warwick puts a quite different interpretation on Hal's association with Falstaff and the tavern set, saying that Hal is educating himself. He mixes with and learns about low life in order to help him later as King. In due time he will reject his tavern companions.

a Find a copy of *Henry IV Part 1* and read Act 1 Scene 2, lines 155–70 to discover how accurately Warwick expresses Hal's intentions.

b How far do you agree with Warwick's general point: that a leader should live with and learn the language and habits of the lowest or worst of his or her followers, in order to lead better ('Turning past-evils to advantages')? See also page 195.

## 2 Very unlikely!

Henry is unconvinced by Warwick's argument. His image in lines 79–80 is from the Bible (Judges 14.8): when a bee builds its honeycomb in the foulest of places ('dead carrion'), it will seldom desert that foul place.

Speak Henry's reply in an appropriate tone of voice, then suggest why Henry is so pessimistic about the possibility of Hal's reform.

---

**unguided days** anarchy
**headstong riot** wilful disorder
**curb** restraint
**lavish manners** loose behaviour
**look beyond** mistake

**gross terms** rude words
**mete** judge
**olive** symbol of peace
**every course ... particular** detail

The blood weeps from my heart when I do shape
In forms imaginary th'unguided days
And rotten times that you shall look upon                    60
When I am sleeping with my ancestors.
For when his headstrong riot hath no curb,
When rage and hot blood are his counsellors,
When means and lavish manners meet together,
O, with what wings shall his affections fly                  65
Towards fronting peril and opposed decay!
WARWICK  My gracious lord, you look beyond him quite:
The prince but studies his companions
Like a strange tongue, wherein, to gain the language,
'Tis needful that the most immodest word                    70
Be looked upon and learnt; which once attained,
Your highness knows comes to no further use
But to be known and hated. So, like gross terms,
The prince will in the perfectness of time
Cast off his followers, and their memory                    75
Shall as a pattern or a measure live
By which his grace must mete the lives of other,
Turning past-evils to advantages.
KING  'Tis seldom when the bee doth leave her comb
In the dead carrion.

            *Enter* WESTMORELAND

                Who's here, Westmoreland?                    80
WESTMORELAND  Health to my sovereign, and new happiness
Added to that that I am to deliver.
Prince John your son doth kiss your grace's hand:
Mowbray, the Bishop Scroop, Hastings and all
Are brought to the correction of your law.                  85
There is not now a rebel's sword unsheathed,
But Peace puts forth her olive everywhere.
The manner how this action hath been borne
Here at more leisure may your highness read,
With every course in his particular.                        90

*For King Henry, Westmoreland's news is as welcome as spring.*
*Harcourt brings news of Northumberland's defeat, but Henry suffers a*
*sudden collapse. Gloucester tells of ominous happenings in nature.*

## 1 Who is Harcourt?

This is Harcourt's only appearance in the play and he speaks only the
eight lines opposite. His dramatic function seems merely to bring news
of the rebels' defeat. Harcourt gives you an opportunity to view the
play from a different point of view. Step into his shoes, and invent a
personality and position for yourself. Tell your story of how you came
to be at the battle of Bramham Moor at which Northumberland and
Lord Bardolph were defeated. What do you know about earlier events
in the play?

## 2 Nature as omen (in pairs)

In a number of his plays (for example, *Julius Caesar* and *Macbeth*),
Shakespeare dramatised the popular belief that the imminent death of
kings was predicted by violent disturbances in nature. In lines 121–8,
Gloucester and Clarence recount the natural disorders that they think
foretell King Henry's death. An actor who played Gloucester said:

> 'It's important in speaking these lines not to fall into a doom-laden tone
> of voice. There are much more effective ways of speaking.'

Use his advice to explore different styles of delivery.

## 3 Shakespeare and history

The Gaultree Forest episode took place in 1405, the battle of Bramham
Moor in 1408, and Henry's death in 1413. Here Shakespeare presents
them happening very closely together in time. To find how Shakespeare
creates his own version of history for dramatic purposes, turn to
page 202.

---

| | |
|---|---|
| **haunch** end | **wrought the mure** built the wall |
| **lifting up** lengthening | **fear me** worry (or frighten) me |
| (the promise of spring) | **Unfathered heirs** children born of |
| **shrieve** sheriff | virgins |
| **whet** sharpen, give a cutting edge to | **loathly** monstrous |
| **stomach** appetite | |

KING  O Westmoreland, thou art a summer bird,
       Which ever in the haunch of winter sings
       The lifting up of day.

*Enter* HARCOURT

                  Look, here's more news.
HARCOURT  From enemies heavens keep your majesty,
       And when they stand against you, may they fall       95
       As those that I am come to tell you of.
       The Earl Northumberland, and the Lord Bardolph,
       With a great power of English, and of Scots,
       Are by the shrieve of Yorkshire overthrown.
       The manner and true order of the fight       100
       This packet, please it you, contains at large.
KING  And wherefore should these good news make me sick?
       Will Fortune never come with both hands full,
       But whet her fair words still in foulest terms?
       She either gives a stomach and no food –       105
       Such are the poor, in health – or else a feast
       And takes away the stomach – such are the rich
       That have abundance and enjoy it not.
       I should rejoice now at this happy news,
       And now my sight fails, and my brain is giddy.       110
       O me, come near me, now I am much ill.
GLOUCESTER  Comfort your majesty.
CLARENCE                  O my royal father!
WESTMORELAND  My sovereign lord, cheer up yourself, look up.
WARWICK  Be patient, princes, you do know these fits
       Are with his highness very ordinary.       115
       Stand from him, give him air: he'll straight be well.
CLARENCE  No, no, he cannot long hold out these pangs;
       Th'incessant care and labour of his mind
       Hath wrought the mure that should confine it in
       So thin that life looks through.       120
GLOUCESTER  The people fear me, for they do observe
       Unfathered heirs and loathly births of nature.
       The seasons change their manners, as the year
       Had found some months asleep and leaped them over.

*Clarence reports further ominous natural events. The crown is set on the pillow beside the sick King Henry. Hal, left alone with his father, reflects on the cares of kingship.*

## 1 Moving the king (in small groups)

The stage direction *'The King is laid on a bed'* sets a very practical problem: how to perform the action of the sick king being moved from his chair (see stage direction at the opening of the scene) to a bed? In different productions, the bed has been placed variously at the front, back and side of the stage. Many editions of the play begin a new scene, in a different location, at line 133.

How would you stage it? Work out how to carry out the move so that the audience's attention is never lost.

## 2 'Enter Prince Henry'

Hal is cheerful when he enters. At what point do you think his mood changes? Identify the line in the script, and suggest how Hal reacts when he realises that his father is very seriously ill.

## 3 Sleep (in pairs)

Hal seems amazed that King Henry can sleep so soundly. He reflects that the cares of monarchy bring sleeplessness. But even when sleep comes, a king does not sleep as soundly as a humble peasant.

Compare lines 153–8 with King Henry's soliloquy on sleep in Act 3 Scene 1, lines 4–31. Experiment with ways of speaking the two soliloquies so that one echoes the other.

Does Hal speak 'sleep with it now!' as an amazed exclamation, or as an imperative (a kind of order to his father to sleep soundly)?

---

**river** Thames
**Time's doting chronicles** who love telling old tales
**Edward** King Edward III (see family tree in *Part 1*, Cambridge School Shakespeare, page 1)

**dull** quiet
**heaviness** sadness
**physic** medicine
**perturbation** disquiet, anxiety, agitation
**ports** eyes
**biggen** nightcap

CLARENCE  The river hath thrice flowed, no ebb between,          125
        And the old folks – Time's doting chronicles –
        Say it did so a little time before
        That our great-grandsire Edward sicked and died.
WARWICK  Speak lower, princes, for the king recovers.
GLOUCESTER  This apoplexy will certain be his end.          130
KING  I pray you take me up and bear me hence
        Into some other chamber.
                *[The King is laid on a bed]*
        Let there be no noise made, my gentle friends,
        Unless some dull and favourable hand
        Will whisper music to my weary spirit.          135
WARWICK  Call for the music in the other room.
KING  Set me the crown upon my pillow here.
CLARENCE  His eye is hollow, and he changes much.
WARWICK  Less noise, less noise.
              *Enter* PRINCE HENRY
PRINCE                    Who saw the Duke of Clarence?
CLARENCE  I am here, brother, full of heaviness.          140
PRINCE  How now, rain within doors, and none abroad?
        How doth the king?
GLOUCESTER              Exceeding ill.
PRINCE  Heard he the good news yet? Tell it him.
GLOUCESTER  He altered much upon the hearing it.
PRINCE  If he be sick with joy, he'll recover without physic.          145
WARWICK  Not so much noise, my lords; sweet prince,
           speak low,
        The king your father is disposed to sleep.
CLARENCE  Let us withdraw into the other room.
WARWICK  Will't please your grace to go along with us?
PRINCE  No, I will sit and watch here by the king.          150
                *[Exeunt all but the Prince]*
        Why doth the crown lie there upon his pillow
        Being so troublesome a bedfellow?
        O polished perturbation! Golden care!
        That keep'st the ports of slumber open wide
        To many a watchful night – sleep with it now!          155
        Yet not so sound, and half so deeply sweet
        As he whose brow, with homely biggen bound,
        Snores out the watch of night. O majesty!

*Hal fears his father is dead. He vows to grieve. Taking the crown,*
*he swears to guard it and to pass it to his own successors.*
*Hal leaves the room. The king wakes.*

Hal takes the crown. A stage convention is that a character always tells the truth in soliloquy. Is Hal totally sincere in all he says? Explore different ways of speaking lines 151–77.

## 1 Were they listening?

How quickly do Warwick, Gloucester and Clarence respond to King Henry's call? Might they have been listening outside the chamber?

---

**scald'st with safety** torments and protects
**gates of breath** lips
**suspire** breathe
**rigol** circle, crown
**due** debt, entitlement
**filial** son-like

**immediate** next in line
**Derives** descends
**put … strength** if all the world were put
**lineal** inherited
**liege** lord

When thou dost pinch thy bearer, thou dost sit
Like a rich armour worn in heat of day,                    160
That scald'st with safety; by his gates of breath
There lies a downy feather which stirs not:
Did he suspire, that light and weightless down
Perforce must move. My gracious lord, my father!
This sleep is sound indeed, this is a sleep                165
That from this golden rigol hath divorced
So many English kings. Thy due from me
Is tears and heavy sorrows of the blood,
Which nature, love, and filial tenderness
Shall, O dear father, pay thee plenteously.                170
My due from thee is this imperial crown
Which, as immediate from thy place and blood,
Derives itself to me. Lo where it sits,

*[Putting it on his head]*

Which God shall guard; and, put the world's whole strength
Into one giant arm, it shall not force                     175
This lineal honour from me: this from thee
Will I to mine leave, as 'tis left to me.

*Exit*

KING  Warwick, Gloucester, Clarence!

*Enter* WARWICK, GLOUCESTER, CLARENCE

CLARENCE  Doth the king call?
WARWICK                    What would your majesty?
KING  Why did you leave me here alone, my lords?          180
CLARENCE  We left the prince my brother here, my liege,
    Who undertook to sit and watch by you.
KING  The Prince of Wales? Where is he? Let me see him.
    He is not here.
WARWICK  This door is open: he is gone this way.          185
GLOUCESTER  He came not through the chamber where we stayed.
KING  Where is the crown? Who took it from my pillow?
WARWICK  When we withdrew, my liege, we left it there.

*King Henry thinks the worst of Hal's action in taking the crown.*
*He reflects bitterly how sons will kill their fathers for their wealth.*
*Warwick reports that Hal was grieving deeply.*

## 1 Contempt and irony? (in pairs)

King Henry is grievously ill, but is bitter about what he thinks is Hal's callous and greedy action. Speak lines 189–210, remembering that Henry thinks that his son cannot wait for him to die, but wants all his wealth and power now. An actor who played Henry said:

> 'The key to the speech is the three passionate repetitions of "For this". Henry tries to get all the contempt he can into these two words, because for him they symbolise Hal's betrayal (indeed, all sons' betrayal of their fathers). All three repetitions lead up to the savagely spoken "When" as he gives the ironic example of the bee.'

## 2 Does it matter? (in pairs)

Give your reply to someone who says 'Henry or Shakespeare seem to muddle up different bees. Worker bees bring honey to the hive, but it is the drones who are killed.'

## 3 'Strange-achievèd gold'

No one is quite sure what Shakespeare had in mind when he wrote 'strange-achievèd gold' (line 201). Make a suggestion of your own in addition to the two given at the foot of the page. Is Henry remembering that his own crown was doubtfully achieved?

## 4 Personification

Consider the three examples of personification opposite: 'Nature' (line 195), 'Sickness' (line 210), 'tyranny' (line 214). Put them in order of the vividness and clarity of pictures they call up in your mind.

---

**part** action
**industry** hard work
**engrossèd and pilled up** collected and pillaged
**strange-achievèd** hard won, doubtfully acquired

**invest** instruct, endow
**martial** military
**engrossments** results, harvest
**ending** dying
**determined** killed, ended
**quaffed** drank

KING   The prince hath ta'en it hence. Go seek him out.  
        Is he so hasty, that he doth suppose            190  
        My sleep my death?  
        Find him, my Lord of Warwick, chide him hither.

                                *[Exit Warwick]*

        This part of his conjoins with my disease  
        And helps to end me. See, sons, what things you are,  
        How quickly Nature falls into revolt            195  
        When gold becomes her object!  
        For this the foolish over-careful fathers  
        Have broke their sleep with thoughts,  
        Their brains with care, their bones with industry;  
        For this they have engrossèd and pilled up       200  
        The cankered heaps of strange-achievèd gold;  
        For this they have been thoughtful to invest  
        Their sons with arts and martial exercises,  
        When like the bee tolling from every flower,  
        Our thighs packed with wax, our mouths with honey,   205  
        We bring it to the hive; and like the bees  
        Are murdered for our pains. This bitter taste  
        Yields his engrossments to the ending father.

                   *Enter* WARWICK

        Now where is he that will not stay so long  
        Till his friend Sickness' hands determined me?     210  
WARWICK   My lord, I found the prince in the next room,  
        Washing with kindly tears his gentle cheeks,  
        With such a deep demeanour in great sorrow  
        That tyranny, which never quaffed but blood,  
        Would, by beholding him, have washed his knife    215  
        With gentle eye-drops. He is coming hither.  
KING   But wherefore did he take away the crown?

             *Enter* PRINCE HENRY

        Lo where he comes. Come hither to me, Harry.  
        Depart the chamber, leave us here alone.

           *Exeunt [Gloucester, Clarence, Warwick]*

PRINCE   I never thought to hear you speak again.         220

*King Henry accuses Hal of impatiently wanting him dead. His belief that Hal never loved him is proved true. He predicts the chaos that will follow when Hal is king.*

## 1 Enact Henry's accusations (in groups of any size)

On stage, Henry lies in bed speaking lines 221–66 to Hal. There are few actions. In the classroom, the lines offer opportunities for dramatic enactment that help understanding by physically portraying the many examples of disorder that Henry lists. Here are two examples:

a One person plays Hal, all the others are King Henry. Hal stands or sits in the centre of a circle of Henrys. Each Henry speaks a short section of the script in turn, accompanying the words with an action of some kind. Hal has to turn to face each speaker and repeat the action.

b One person speaks Henry's lines, pausing after each short section (for example, a line or phrase – 'Dost thou so hunger for mine empty chair', or even a single word – 'dance'). In the pause, the others enact the words. The mimes can be any imaginative action triggered by the language.

## 2 The wish is father to the thought (in small groups)

In line 220, Hal says that he thought his father to be dead. Henry's reply (line 221) has become a well-known proverb meaning that you think, see or hear what you want to think, see or hear.

Give a few examples from your own personal experience that confirm or deny the proverb. Then discuss the claims that:

- All religions are based on this proverb.
- All political ideologies are based on this proverb.
- The proverb applies more to King Henry than it does to Hal.

---

**cloud of dignity** feeble royalty
**sealed up** fulfilled
**manifest** show
**whetted** sharpened
**bedew** moisten, damp
**balm** holy oil
**compound** mix

**decrees** laws
**Form** order
**Vanity** worthlessness (Falstaff)
**sage** wise
**neighbour confines** bordering countries
**double gild** thickly cover, adorn

KING  Thy wish was father, Harry, to that thought.
      I stay too long by thee, I weary thee.
      Dost thou so hunger for mine empty chair
      That thou wilt needs invest thee with my honours
      Before the hour be ripe? O foolish youth,         225
      Thou seek'st the greatness that will overwhelm thee.
      Stay but a little, for my cloud of dignity
      Is held from falling with so weak a wind
      That it will quickly drop: my day is dim.
      Thou hast stol'n that which after some few hours     230
      Were thine without offence, and at my death
      Thou hast sealed up my expectation.
      Thy life did manifest thou lovedst me not,
      And thou wilt have me die assured of it.
      Thou hidst a thousand daggers in thy thoughts,     235
      Whom thou hast whetted on thy stony heart
      To stab at half an hour of my life.
      What, canst thou not forbear me half an hour?
      Then get thee gone, and dig my grave thyself,
      And bid the merry bells ring to thine ear        240
      That thou art crownèd, not that I am dead.
      Let all the tears that should bedew my hearse
      Be drops of balm to sanctify thy head:
      Only compound me with forgotten dust.
      Give that which gave thee life unto the worms,     245
      Pluck down my officers, break my decrees,
      For now a time is come to mock at Form:
      Harry the fifth is crowned, up, Vanity,
      Down, royal state, all you sage counsellors, hence!
      And to the English court assemble now         250
      From every region, apes of idleness!
      Now, neighbour confines, purge you of your scum.
      Have you a ruffian that will swear, drink, dance,
      Revel the night, rob, murder, and commit
      The oldest sins the newest kind of ways?        255
      Be happy, he will trouble you no more:
      England shall double gild his treble guilt,
      England shall give him office, honour, might;

*King Henry fears that England, ruled by his son, will descend into savagery. Hal returns the crown, wishing Henry long life, and explaining how he cursed the crown for killing his father.*

## 1 England under Henry V (in pairs)

King Henry paints a vivid picture of England fallen into anarchy when his son is king. As one person speaks lines 246–66, the other person echoes every word that contributes to a sense of disorder, violence and corruption ('Pluck', 'break', 'mock', and so on).

## 2 Hal explains all (individually or in groups)

An actor who played Hal offered this advice on speaking lines 267–305:

> 'Because Hal is utterly sincere, you have to speak quietly and reasonably. He feels deeply, but he keeps his emotions tightly under control as he carefully explains his motives and actions.'

Speak Hal's explanation yourself, or work in a group and share out the lines. Use the following summary to help you:

> 'Grief prevented me from interrupting your rebuke. Here is the crown, may God guard your possession of it, and may God witness my desire that you should possess it honourably. If I lie ("feign"), may I not live to fulfil my intention to reject my former way of life.
> 'I rebuked the crown as worse than gold that could be used as medicine ("med'cine potable"), and had killed its wearer. I regarded the crown as an enemy that it was my duty to oppose because it had murdered my father. If any feeling of joy or pride at the prospect of becoming king enter my mind, I hope never to succeed to the throne.'

After you have spoken Hal's lines, say whether you agree with the actor's judgement that Hal is sincere.

---

**curbed licence** restrained debauchery
**muzzle** protective harness
**flesh his tooth** bite and devour
**impediments** obstructions
**forestalled** prevented
**affect** aspire to

**prostrate and exterior bending** humble kneeling
**incredulous** unbelieving
**on thee depending** that hangs on you
**carat** quality
**try** struggle, fight

For the fifth Harry from curbed licence plucks
The muzzle of restraint, and the wild dog                        260
Shall flesh his tooth on every innocent.
O my poor kingdom! Sick with civil blows,
When that my care could not withhold thy riots
What wilt thou do when riot is thy care?
O, thou wilt be a wilderness again,                              265
Peopled with wolves, thy old inhabitants.

PRINCE  O, pardon me, my liege. But for my tears,
The moist impediments unto my speech,
I had forestalled this dear and deep rebuke
Ere you with grief had spoke, and I had heard               270
The course of it so far. There is your crown;
And He that wears the crown immortally
Long guard it yours. If I affect it more
Than as your honour and as your renown,
Let me no more from this obedience rise,                        275
Which my most inward true and duteous spirit
Teacheth this prostrate and exterior bending,
God witness with me. When I here came in
And found no course of breath within your majesty,
How cold it struck my heart! If I do feign,                      280
O, let me in my present wildness die,
And never live to show th'incredulous world
The noble change that I have purposèd.
Coming to look on you, thinking you dead,
And dead almost, my liege, to think you were,             285
I spake unto this crown as having sense,
And thus upbraided it: 'The care on thee depending
Hath fed upon the body of my father;
Therefore thou best of gold art worse than gold,
Other, less fine, in carat more precious,                         290
Preserving life in med'cine potable;
But thou, most fine, most honoured, most renowned,
Hast eat thy bearer up.' Thus, my most royal liege,
Accusing it, I put it on my head,
To try with it, as with an enemy                                    295
That had before my face murdered my father,
The quarrel of a true inheritor.

*Hal denies feeling joy or pride in wearing the crown. Henry accepts Hal's explanation, and admits his own doubtful right to be king. He says that Hal's claim to the crown is firmer, but warns of dangers.*

## 1 A rightful king? (in small groups)

Henry is reconciled with his son, and hopes that Hal's claim to the throne will be much stronger than his own. He advises that the way to unite the different factions in England is to rally them to fight against a common, foreign enemy. Work together on some of the following:

a *Henry the usurper.* Henry's admission of the 'by-paths and indirect crooked ways' by which he became king recall the events that Shakespeare dramatised in *Richard II*. Turn to page 1 to remind yourself of how Henry became king.

b *Choice of language.* Henry says he 'met' the crown (line 313), which sounds as if he simply found it, rather than admitting the very active part in toppling King Richard II. What is your reaction to his use of 'purchased' in line 327?

c *A better claim?* Hal will succeed to the throne as King Henry V. But does that give him a better title to the throne than his father who usurped it? Give your reply.

d *A theatrical metaphor.* In lines 325–6, Henry says:

'For all my reign hath been but as a scene
Acting that argument'

Like 'scene' and 'acting', 'argument' is a theatrical term. It is the summary of the plot added at the beginning of the published script of a play. When you have read to the end of the play write your own 'argument' of it in not more than two sentences (see page 190).

---

| | |
|---|---|
| **vassal** slave | **supposèd** the pretence of |
| **quiet/… opinion … confirmation** | **more fairer sort** better justified |
| peace … reputation … legitimacy | manner |
| **soil of the achievement** moral | **garland** crown |
| stains of my becoming king | **green** fresh |
| **with boisterous hand** roughly | **fell** violent |

But if it did infect my blood with joy,
Or swell my thoughts to any strain of pride,
If any rebel or vain spirit of mine                                    300
Did with the least affection of a welcome
Give entertainment to the might of it,
Let God for ever keep it from my head,
And make me as the poorest vassal is
That doth with awe and terror kneel to it.                             305

KING   God put in thy mind to take it hence,
That thou mightst win the more thy father's love,
Pleading so wisely in excuse of it.
Come hither, Harry, sit thou by my bed,
And hear, I think, the very latest counsel                             310
That ever I shall breathe. God knows, my son,
By what by-paths and indirect crooked ways
I met this crown, and I myself know well
How troublesome it sat upon my head.
To thee it shall descend with better quiet,                            315
Better opinion, better confirmation,
For all the soil of the achievement goes
With me into the earth. It seemed in me
But as an honour snatched with boisterous hand,
And I had many living to upbraid                                       320
My gain of it by their assistances,
Which daily grew to quarrel and to bloodshed,
Wounding supposèd peace. All these bold fears
Thou seest with peril I have answerèd,
For all my reign hath been but as a scene                              325
Acting that argument; and now my death
Changes the mood, for what in me was purchased
Falls upon thee in a more fairer sort.
So thou the garland wear'st successively,
Yet though thou stand'st more sure than I could do,                    330
Thou art not firm enough since griefs are green,
And all my friends, which thou must make thy friends,
Have but their stings and teeth newly ta'en out,
By whose fell working I was first advanced,
And by whose power I well might lodge a fear                           335
To be again displaced; which to avoid
I cut them off, and had a purpose now
To lead out many to the Holy Land,

*Henry reveals that his motive for the crusade was to prevent enquiry into how he became king. He advises Hal to fight foreign wars to unite possible rebels. He resolves for death in the Jerusalem Chamber.*

## 1 Good advice? (in small groups)

In Shakespeare's *Henry V*, Hal shows how he takes his father's advice to 'busy giddy minds / With foreign quarrels'. As King Henry V, he leads an army of English, Welsh, Scots and Irish to fight against the French. Talk together about what you think of the following claim by a politician:

> 'Henry's advice, to "busy giddy minds with foreign quarrels" should be the major guiding principle of any politician. People are always united by having a common enemy who is visibly different from themselves.'

## 2 King Henry's troubled conscience

Look back over lines 311–47 and pick out all the language that Henry uses to admit the weakness of his right to rule as king.

## 3 Rhymes (in pairs)

Lines 346–51 are written in rhyming couplets. Speak the lines in two ways. First, stress the rhythms and rhymes very emphatically. Second, speak in a less formal manner, not stressing the rhymes. Which style seems more appropriate?

## 4 Jerusalem

a Henry may not live to lead a crusade to the Holy Land, but he will die in the Jerusalem Chamber. Does he speak his final lines with ironic amusement or in some other way?

b This edition sets the whole of Scene 2 in the Jerusalem Chamber. Turn back to Activity 1 on page 142 to find a way of making sense of lines 366–7.

---

**still** always
**look/Too near** research carefully
**giddy minds** rebellious factions

**waste** erase, weaken
**period** stop
**Laud** praise

Lest rest and lying still might make them look
Too near unto my state. Therefore, my Harry,    340
Be it thy course to busy giddy minds
With foreign quarrels, that action hence borne out
May waste the memory of the former days.
More would I, but my lungs are wasted so
That strength of speech is utterly denied me.    345
How I came by the crown, O God forgive,
And grant it may with thee in true peace live.
PRINCE  You won it, wore it, kept it, gave it me:
Then plain and right must my possession be,
Which I with more than with a common pain    350
'Gainst all the world will rightfully maintain.

*Enter Lord* JOHN *of Lancaster*

KING  Look, look, here comes my John of Lancaster.
JOHN  Health, peace and happiness to my royal father.
KING  Thou bring'st me happiness and peace, son John,
But health, alack, with youthful wings is flown    355
From this bare withered trunk. Upon thy sight
My worldly business makes a period.
Where is my Lord of Warwick?
PRINCE                  My Lord of Warwick!

[*Enter* WARWICK]

KING  Doth any name particular belong
Unto the lodging where I first did swoon?    360
WARWICK  'Tis called Jerusalem, my noble lord.
KING  Laud be to God, even there my life must end.
It hath been prophesied to me, many years,
I should not die but in Jerusalem,
Which vainly I supposed the Holy Land.    365
But bear me to that chamber, there I'll lie:
In that Jerusalem shall Harry die.

*Exeunt*

# Looking back at Act 4
*Activities for groups or individuals*

## 1 Judging Prince John

Prince John deliberately lies in order to trick the rebel leaders into dismissing their army. Modern audiences usually see John as calculating and deceitful, but many members of Shakespeare's Elizabethan audience saw his action justified in at least two ways:

- The Divine Right of Kings held that the king was God's deputy on earth. To rebel against the king was to rebel against God, and so any action to defeat rebellion was just.

- Machiavelli's *The Prince* was a very influential book on government which argued that a ruler could be deceitful or unjust and use any bad means in order to hang on to power for the good of the state (see page 192, 'Policy').

What do you think of Prince John falsely giving his word of honour in order to defeat the rebels? Take roles (for example, as John, Shakespeare, Machiavelli, a modern political leader – and yourself), and argue what you think of John's behaviour in Gaultree Forest.

## 2 Speaking Shakespeare: a 'special' voice?

Many people used to think that Shakespeare's 'noble' characters should always speak in the 'Received Pronunciation' (RP) accent of the English upper-middle class of the early twentieth century. Today, few people believe that. They argue that Shakespeare's own actors did not speak in such a way, and that what really matters is that (for example) a king should usually have a tone of authority in his voice. An accent (which simply means a particular way of speaking) can be used to add to dramatic effect.

How do you think the characters in this act should speak? Select two characters from each scene and speak some of their lines. What qualities should they have in their voices?

## 3 Court circular

Today, a Court circular briefly describes the activity of all members of the Royal family over a short period of time. Write the Court circular for Act 4.

Choose a line from Scene 2 as a suitable caption for this picture.

## 4 The people of England

There are no women in Act 4, and the 'ordinary' people of England appear only as soldiers in Scene 1 and as court attendants in Scene 2. Give them a voice by inventing a character for each scene who comments on what the aristocrats have done.

## 5 Costume design

Use clues from the script to design costumes for Westmoreland, the Archbishop, Falstaff, King Henry and Hal.

*Shallow insists that Falstaff stay the night. Davy and Shallow discuss supper, and legal and farm matters. Shallow, hoping to gain from Falstaff's friendship, tells Davy to treat Falstaff's men well.*

## 1 Rural life (in small groups)

Every production of the play tries to create a strong sense of rural life, partly through set, lighting and sometimes music. But the language itself evokes a bustling country world (hade land, red wheat, pigeons, smith, and so on).

Take parts as Shallow, Falstaff, Davy, Bardolph and the Page (who does not speak). Rehearse and act out the scene. Use the following to help you increase the humour of the scene and to explore the relationship of Shallow and Davy:

*Shallow* has the habit of often repeating himself, and is determined to be a good host to Falstaff (who might gain him favours at Court). Does he speak lines 25–7 out of Falstaff's hearing?

*Davy* has been in Shallow's employment for eight years, and organises his household and farm. He keeps Shallow informed about legal ('precepts' are writs or summons to court), domestic and farm matters ('hade land' is headland, a strip of land where the plough turned). Is he like Shallow in appearance and manner? Does he speak to Shallow like a respectful servant, or in some other manner?

## 2 Davy's list

Imagine Davy carries a list of all the things about which he wishes to remind Shallow. Write out his list, with notes about what outcomes Davy would prefer.

---

**cock and pie** a mild oath
**smith's note** blacksmith's invoice
**cast** added up
**link** chain, rope
**Hinckley Fair** famous fair near Coventry each 26 August
**A shall answer** he must pay

**kickshaws** fancy extras
**man of war** soldier, Falstaff
**arrant** notorious
**backbite** speak ill behind your back
**foul linen** lousy shirts
**Well conceited** very witty

# Gloucestershire: Justice Shallow's house


*Enter* SHALLOW, FALSTAFF, BARDOLPH *and* PAGE

SHALLOW  By cock and pie, sir, you shall not away tonight. – What, Davy
I say!

FALSTAFF  You must excuse me, Master Robert Shallow.

SHALLOW  I will not excuse you, you shall not be excused, excuses shall
not be admitted, there is no excuse shall serve, you shall not be     5
excused. – Why, Davy!

[*Enter* DAVY]

DAVY  Here, sir.

SHALLOW  Davy, Davy, Davy, Davy, let me see, Davy, let me see, Davy,
let me see – Yea marry, William cook, bid him come hither. – Sir
John, you shall not be excused.     10

DAVY  Marry, sir, thus: those precepts cannot be served; and again, sir:
shall we sow the hade land with wheat?

SHALLOW  With red wheat, Davy. But for William cook – are there no
young pigeons?

DAVY  Yes, sir. Here is now the smith's note for shoeing and     15
plough-irons.

SHALLOW  Let it be cast and paid. – Sir John, you shall not be excused.

DAVY  Now, sir, a new link to the bucket must needs be had. And, sir, do
you mean to stop any of William's wages about the sack he lost at
Hinckley Fair?     20

SHALLOW  A shall answer it. – Some pigeons, Davy, a couple of
shortlegged hens, a joint of mutton, and any pretty little tiny
kickshaws, tell William cook.

DAVY  Doth the man of war stay all night, sir?

SHALLOW  Yea, Davy. I will use him well, a friend i'th'court is better than     25
a penny in purse. Use his men well, Davy, for they are arrant knaves
and will backbite.

DAVY  No worse than they are back-bitten, sir, for they have marvellous
foul linen.

SHALLOW  Well conceited, Davy. About your business, Davy.     30

*Davy pleads for Shallow to favour his friend in a lawsuit. Falstaff reflects how Shallow and his servants resemble each other, and how Hal will laugh when Falstaff tells tales of Shallow.*

## 1 Rural justice (in pairs)

Davy puts in a word for his friend William Visor who is due to appear before Justice Shallow because of a complaint by Clement Perkes ('countenance' means 'favour'). No one knows why Shakespeare put Visor and Perkes into the play. Some people argue that he knew families of that name living at Woodmancote ('Woncot') in Gloucestershire.

Suggest one or two reasons why Shakespeare inserted this little episode into the play. For example, how might it relate to other characters or themes?

## 2 Irony? (in groups of three)

> 'It is certain that either wise bearing or ignorant carriage is caught, as
> men take diseases, one of another. Therefore let men take heed of their
> company' (lines 59–62).

Take roles as Falstaff, Hal and King Henry. Let each character speak in turn, saying how these lines about Shallow and Davy apply to their own relationships. Then each person gives their own personal views on the lines.

## 3 An Inn-joke?

Shakespeare may have included lines 63–5 as a private joke for lawyers and law students at the Inns of Court. A legal year was divided into four terms, with intervallums (recesses, vacations) between. A legal action often lasted for two terms.

---

**staves** thin poles
**semblable coherence** visible
  similarity
**the participation of society**
  living together

**suit to** favour to ask
**imputation** claim
**curry with** flatter
**bearing ... carriage** behaviour
**ill laid up** flung in a heap

DAVY  I beseech you, sir, to countenance William Visor of Woncot against Clement Perkes a'th'Hill.

SHALLOW  There is many complaints, Davy, against that Visor – that Visor is an arrant knave, on my knowledge.

DAVY  I grant your worship that he is a knave, sir; but yet God forbid, sir, 35 but a knave should have some countenance at his friend's request. An honest man, sir, is able to speak for himself, when a knave is not. I have served your worship truly, sir, this eight years and if I cannot once or twice in a quarter bear out a knave against an honest man, I have little credit with your worship. The knave is mine honest 40 friend, sir, therefore I beseech you let him be countenanced.

SHALLOW  Go to, I say, he shall have no wrong. Look about, Davy.

                                                *[Exit Davy]*
– Where are you, Sir John? Come, come, come, off with your boots. Give me your hand, Master Bardolph.

BARDOLPH  I am glad to see your worship.                              45

SHALLOW  I thank thee with my heart, kind Master Bardolph; *[To the Page]* and welcome, my tall fellow. – Come, Sir John.

FALSTAFF  I'll follow you, good Master Shallow.

                                                *[Exit Shallow]*
Bardolph, look to our horses.          *[Exit Bardolph with Page]*
If I were sawed into quantities, I should make four dozen of such 50 bearded hermits' staves as Master Shallow. It is a wonderful thing to see the semblable coherence of his men's spirits and his: they by observing him do bear themselves like foolish justices; he by conversing with them is turned into a justice-like servingman. Their spirits are so married in conjunction, with the participation of society, 55 that they flock together in consent like so many wild geese. If I had a suit to Master Shallow, I would humour his men with the imputation of being near their master; if to his men, I would curry with Master Shallow, that no man could better command his servants. It is certain that either wise bearing or ignorant carriage is caught, as men take 60 diseases, one of another. Therefore let men take heed of their company. I will devise matter enough out of this Shallow to keep Prince Harry in continual laughter the wearing out of six fashions – which is four terms – or two actions, and a shall laugh without intervallums. O, it is much that a lie with a slight oath and a jest with a 65 sad brow will do with a fellow that never had the ache in his shoulders! O, you shall see him laugh till his face be like a wet cloak ill laid up.

SHALLOW  *[Within]* Sir John!

FALSTAFF  I come, Master Shallow, I come, Master Shallow.        *Exit*

*King Henry IV is dead, and the Lord Chief Justice and Warwick fear the future under Hal, now King Henry V. The Justice is prepared for the worst, and Warwick foresees villainous people taking power.*

## 1 Fear and foreboding (in groups of six)

One person acts as director. The others take parts as the characters who speak lines 1–41. Your task at the opening of Scene 2 is to create a feeling of anxiety and fear.

Hal has now succeeded to the throne as King Henry V. Everyone expects that he will continue in his wild and riotous ways and that England is about to sink into anarchy.

The Lord Chief Justice, who had once imprisoned Hal, is resigned to 'all injuries' (punishments). Hal's three brothers grieve for their dead father, but in lines 27–34 show that they too think that Hal's corrupt tavern associates will come to power in England.

The person acting as director guides the actors through the lines, suggesting how they could speak and move to help create the climate of unease.

## 2 'The worst'?

Warwick wishes that Hal was at least as good as the worst of his three brothers (lines 15–16) because he fears that 'spirits of vile sort' will take over the high offices of state from the nobles who now hold them. But how does Warwick speak his lines without offending the brother he describes as 'the worst'?

Imagine you are Warwick. Which brother do you have in mind? Just how do you deliver the lines without giving offence?

---

**truly** in good faith
**condition of the time** whatever time may bring, disturbed nature of the times
**fantasy** wildest imaginings

**heavy issue** sad children
**temper** temperament
**strike sail ... sort!** submit to corrupt people

# ACT 5   SCENE 2
## London: the Palace of Westminster


*Enter the Earl of* WARWICK *and the* LORD CHIEF JUSTICE

WARWICK  How now, my Lord Chief Justice, whither away?
JUSTICE  How doth the king?
WARWICK  Exceeding well: his cares are now all ended.
JUSTICE  I hope, not dead.
WARWICK              He's walked the way of nature,
    And to our purposes he lives no more.                                   5
JUSTICE  I would his majesty had called me with him:
    The service that I truly did his life
    Hath left me open to all injuries.
WARWICK  Indeed I think the young king loves you not.
JUSTICE  I know he doth not, and do arm myself                              10
    To welcome the condition of the time,
    Which cannot look more hideously upon me
    Than I have drawn it in my fantasy.

*Enter [Prince]* JOHN *of Lancaster,* GLOUCESTER *and* CLARENCE

WARWICK  Here come the heavy issue of dead Harry.
    O, that the living Harry had the temper                              15
    Of he, the worst of these three gentlemen!
    How many nobles then should hold their places,
    That must strike sail to spirits of vile sort!
JUSTICE  O God, I fear all will be overturned.
JOHN  Good morrow, cousin Warwick, good morrow.                             20
GLOUCESTER *and* CLARENCE  Good morrow, cousin.
JOHN  We meet like men that had forgot to speak.
WARWICK  We do remember, but our argument
    Is all too heavy to admit much talk.
JOHN  Well, peace be with him that hath made us heavy.                      25
JUSTICE  Peace be with us, lest we be heavier.

> *The three Dukes see trouble ahead for the Lord Chief Justice.*
> *He says his actions have been just, and he prefers death rather than*
> *dishonour. Hal appears as Henry V, and speaks reassuring words.*

## 1 First words as king (in small groups)

Lines 44–61 are the first words that Hal speaks as King Henry V. He wants to allay the anxieties that his brothers obviously feel, and to win their firm allegiance. Consider each of the following, and speak his lines as convincingly as you can.

a Do his first two lines sound like a rebuke to the Lord Chief Justice's greeting of 'majesty'? Or are they spoken in a different tone?

b An actor playing Hal says to you 'My first speech as king is far too sophisticated and cleverly constructed to be credible to my brothers. How should I speak it?' Give your reply.

c Are they convinced? The brothers reply together (line 62) to Hal's assurance of happiness ahead. But do they believe his promise or do they think he is still the wild and reckless brother they know? Experiment with ways of speaking their reply to find different possibilities.

## 2 'The Turkish court'

Hal recognises that everyone fears what the future will hold in an England ruled by him. Even his brothers suspect they will not be safe. The story that the instant a Turkish sultan came to the throne he killed all his brothers was well known to Elizabethans. It was based on two real instances. In 1574, Sultan Murad III (who was also known as Amrath) had his brothers strangled when he succeeded his father. His successor did the same in 1596.

---

coldest expectation the worst
  hope for the future
speak Sir John Falstaff fair be
  respectful to Falstaff
quality nature

ragged and forestalled remission
  pardon that will not be granted
Harry Harry I (Hal, now Henry
  V) succeed my father (Henry IV)

GLOUCESTER  O good my lord, you have lost a friend indeed,
    And I dare swear you borrow not that face
    Of seeming sorrow: it is sure your own.
JOHN  Though no man be assured what grace to find,   30
    You stand in coldest expectation.
    I am the sorrier, would 'twere otherwise.
CLARENCE  Well, you must now speak Sir John Falstaff fair,
    Which swims against your stream of quality.
JUSTICE  Sweet princes, what I did, I did in honour,   35
    Led by th'impartial conduct of my soul.
    And never shall you see that I will beg
    A ragged and forestalled remission.
    If truth and upright innocency fail me,
    I'll to the king my master that is dead   40
    And tell him who hath sent me after him.

*Enter* PRINCE HENRY *and* BLUNT

WARWICK  Here comes the prince.
JUSTICE  Good morrow, and God save your majesty.
PRINCE  This new and gorgeous garment, majesty,
    Sits not so easy on me as you think.   45
    Brothers, you mix your sadness with some fear.
    This is the English, not the Turkish court:
    Not Amurath an Amurath succeeds,
    But Harry Harry. Yet be sad, good brothers,
    For, by my faith, it very well becomes you.   50
    Sorrow so royally in you appears
    That I will deeply put the fashion on
    And wear it in my heart. Why then, be sad,
    But entertain no more of it, good brothers,
    Than a joint burden laid upon us all.   55
    For me, by Heaven, I bid you be assured
    I'll be your father and your brother too.
    Let me but bear your love, I'll bear your cares.
    Yet weep that Harry's dead, and so will I;
    But Harry lives that shall convert those tears   60
    By number into hours of happiness.
BROTHERS  We hope no otherwise from your majesty.

*Hal asks whether it is possible for him to forget that the Lord Chief Justice imprisoned him. The Justice replies he acted to fulfil the king's law. Would Hal allow a son of his to mock justice?*

## 1 The Justice's defence (in small groups)

Lines 63–4 suggest that Hal's first words as king have not reassured anyone ('strangely' = fearfully). Hal reminds the Lord Chief Justice that he has good cause to be uneasy.

Historically, it is very unlikely that the Justice had once imprisoned Hal, but legend had it that the Prince once boxed the Lord Chief Justice's ears, an offence for which he was sent to prison.

The Lord Chief Justice makes a powerful case to be 'measured rightly' (judged fairly) for his action in punishing Prince Hal. He very carefully builds up his argument, short section by short section, line by line: he represented the king, and carried out his law. When Hal struck him in the court of the King's Bench ('the very seat of judgement') it was an assault upon the king himself.

The Justice asks Hal to imagine a similar case. If Hal, now king, had a son, and that son broke the law, what would he do if the Justice, on the king's behalf ('in your power', line 96), sentenced the son?

Use the following to help you prepare a delivery of the Justice's speech:

- One person speaks the lines slowly, the others echo every word to do with law, justice and authority.
- Speak lines 82–100 ('If the deed ... sovereignty'), emphasising every 'you', 'your' and 'yourself'.
- All the following signify the Lord Chief Justice: 'the person of your father', 'the image of his power', 'image of the king', 'most royal image', 'a second body'.

---

**Lethe** the river of Hades (the underworld) whose waters caused forgetfulness
**presented** represented
**gave bold way to** used the power of
**commit** imprison
**garland** crown

**aweful bench** courts which command respect
**slighted** mocked, rejected
**cold considerance** impartial weighing
**misbecame my place** misused my authority

PRINCE   You all look strangely on me. – And you most:
         You are, I think, assured I love you not.
JUSTICE  I am assured, if I be measured rightly,                        65
         Your majesty hath no just cause to hate me.
PRINCE   No? How might a prince of my great hopes forget
         So great indignities you laid upon me?
         What! Rate, rebuke, and roughly send to prison
         Th'immediate heir of England? Was this easy?                  70
         May this be washed in Lethe and forgotten?
JUSTICE  I then did use the person of your father:
         The image of his power lay then in me;
         And in th'administration of his law,
         Whiles I was busy for the commonwealth,                       75
         Your highness pleasèd to forget my place,
         The majesty and power of law and justice,
         The image of the king whom I presented,
         And struck me in the very seat of judgement;
         Whereon, as an offender to your father,                       80
         I gave bold way to my authority
         And did commit you. If the deed were ill,
         Be you contented, wearing now the garland,
         To have a son set your decrees at nought?
         To pluck down justice from your aweful bench?                 85
         To trip the course of law, and blunt the sword
         That guards the peace and safety of your person?
         Nay, more, to spurn at your most royal image,
         And mock your workings in a second body?
         Question your royal thoughts, make the case yours,            90
         Be now the father and propose a son,
         Hear your own dignity so much profaned,
         See your most dreadful laws so loosely slighted,
         Behold yourself so by a son disdained;
         And then imagine me taking your part,                         95
         And in your power soft silencing your son.
         After this cold considerance, sentence me,
         And, as you are a king, speak in your state
         What I have done that misbecame my place,
         My person, or my liege's sovereignty.                        100

*Hal accepts the Justice's argument and confirms him as Lord Chief Justice and chief adviser. He says all his past wrongdoings are buried with his father, and, reformed, he will reign wisely.*

## 1 The royal 'we'

It was the custom (and still is on formal occasions) of monarchs to refer to themselves as 'we', 'us' and 'our', not 'I' and 'mine'. Find the line in Hal's speech where he shifts from 'I' to 'we' and suggest why his language changes at that particular point.

## 2 Ceremony (in pairs)

In lines 101–20, Hal confirms the Lord Chief Justice as the premier judge in all England. He hands over the Sword of Justice. The sword is still used in coronation ceremonies, handed to the new monarch with the words 'with this sword do justice'.

Take turns to act as Hal and the Lord Chief Justice, speaking the lines and inventing a simple but impressive ceremony to accomapany the words.

## 3 A changed man? (in small groups)

In lines 121–32, Hal announces that he has renounced his former riotous life style. All his past offences are buried with his father. He says he will prove false the prophecies that he will be a bad king. Using an image of the sea flowing and ebbing, he claims his 'vanity' is now changed to 'formal majesty'.

Try different ways of speaking the lines:

- to his brothers and the Lord Chief Justice
- as a speech to a very large crowd
- as a modern Hal, with access to radio and television. Speak the lines as a radio or TV broadcast.

---

**balance and the sword** scales and sword of justice
**father to my youth** (see page 194)
**prompt mine ear** advise me
**gone wild ... affections** buried with all my past passions and misbehaviours

**raze out** erase
**Rotten opinion** vulgar rumours
**seeming** outward appearance
**limbs of noble counsel** wise advisers
**father** Lord Chief Justice

PRINCE  You are right Justice, and you weigh this well.
Therefore still bear the balance and the sword,
And I do wish your honours may increase
Till you do live to see a son of mine
Offend you and obey you as I did.                                   105
So shall I live to speak my father's words:
'Happy am I that have a man so bold
That dares do justice on my proper son;
And not less happy, having such a son
That would deliver up his greatness so.'                            110
Into the hands of Justice you did commit me –
For which I do commit into your hands
Th'unstainèd sword that you have used to bear,
With this remembrance: that you use the same
With the like bold, just, and impartial spirit                      115
As you have done 'gainst me. There is my hand:
You shall be as a father to my youth,
My voice shall sound as you do prompt mine ear,
And I will stoop and humble my intents
To your well-practised wise directions.                             120
And, princes all, believe me, I beseech you,
My father is gone wild into his grave,
For in his tomb lie my affections.
And with his spirits sadly I survive
To mock the expectation of the world,                               125
To frustrate prophecies, and to raze out
Rotten opinion, who hath writ me down
After my seeming. The tide of blood in me
Hath proudly flowed in vanity till now;
Now doth it turn, and ebb back to the sea,                          130
Where it shall mingle with the state of floods,
And flow henceforth in formal majesty.
Now call we our high court of parliament,
And let us choose such limbs of noble counsel
That the great body of our state may go                             135
In equal rank with the best-governed nation;
That war, or peace, or both at once, may be
As things acquainted and familiar to us;
In which you, father, shall have foremost hand.

*Hal proposes to call his nobles together after his coronation and undertakes to rule justly. In his Gloucestershire orchard Shallow entertains Falstaff after supper.*

## 1 A silent comment

Hal looks forward to his reign as a happy time, with God in full support. Many productions stage the king and his nobles leaving the stage with great dignity. However, one production added a silent comment by two servants. They gazed after the departing king and his brothers and shrugged their shoulders in weary resignation as if to say 'But nothing is going to change in our lives'.

What is your reaction to that staging?

## 2 Relaxing after dinner (in small groups)

Justice Shallow has entertained Falstaff, with much wine served at dinner. The men have now retired into Shallow's orchard to eat apples and sweetmeats ('pippins' and 'caraways'). Falstaff comments on Shallow's prosperity, but Shallow waves aside the compliment, saying his land is barren and he is poor.

In this scene, actors often try to create an atmosphere of long-ago rural England: the country squire relaxing in the late evening among his friends. To help your own staging, think about the following:

- Are they drunk? Silence is often played as very tipsy indeed. His bursting into song amazes everyone.

- How much does Falstaff show his true intentions? One production played him as very obviously watching Shallow and Silence, calculating how he might 'fleece' them. His short speeches were contemptuously spoken.

- Davy organises the food and drink ('Spread' = lay the tablecloth). Does he bustle, or shuffle, or …?

---

**accite** summon
**state** nobility
**consigning to** endorsing
**arbour** bower, shady recess
**graffing** grafting
**husband** steward, handyman
**varlet** servant

**quoth a** he said
**flesh** food
**health** toast (Cheers!)
**Proface!** Davy's version of saying grace 'May it do you good'
**bear** endure

Our coronation done, we will accite,                                    140
As I before remembered, all our state,
And, God consigning to my good intents,
No prince nor peer shall have just cause to say:
God shorten Harry's happy life one day.                    *Exeunt*


# ACT 5    SCENE 3
## Gloucestershire: Justice Shallow's orchard


*Enter* FALSTAFF, SHALLOW, SILENCE, DAVY, BARDOLPH, PAGE

SHALLOW  Nay, you shall see my orchard, where, in an arbour, we will eat
  a last year's pippin of mine own graffing, with a dish of caraways,
  and so forth – come, cousin Silence – and then to bed.
FALSTAFF  'Fore God, you have here goodly dwelling, and rich.
SHALLOW  Barren, barren, barren; beggars all, beggars all, Sir John.        5
  Marry, good air. – Spread, Davy, spread, Davy, well said, Davy.
FALSTAFF  This Davy serves you for good uses: he is your servingman
  and your husband.
SHALLOW  A good varlet, a good varlet, a good varlet, Sir John. By the
  Mass, I have drunk too much sack at supper. A good varlet. Now sit    10
  down, now sit down. – Come, cousin.
SILENCE  Ah, sirrah, quoth a, we shall
[*Sings*]  Do nothing but eat and make good cheer,
          And praise God for the merry year,
          When flesh is cheap and females dear,                          15
          And lusty lads roam here and there,
          So merrily,
          And ever among so merrily.
FALSTAFF  There's a merry heart, good Master Silence! I'll give you a
  health for that anon.                                                  20
SHALLOW  Give Master Bardolph some wine, Davy.
DAVY  Sweet sir, sit – I'll be with you anon. Most sweet sir, sit. Master
  page, good master page, sit. Proface! What you want in meat, we'll
  have in drink, but you must bear. The heart's all.          [*Exit*]
SHALLOW  Be merry, Master Bardolph, and my little soldier there, be      25
  merry.

*Silence's singing surprises Falstaff. Davy serves apples and drink, and Bardolph promises to be his friend if one day they meet in London. Someone knocks at the door. Silence sings a drinking song.*

'Now comes in the sweet a'th'night.' Justice Shallow entertains in his Gloucestershire orchard.

## 1 Drinking songs (in pairs)

Silence's snatches of drinking songs provide great opportunities for an actor to create a memorable character. In lines 42–3, he promises to drink to the bottom of his tankard, even if it is a mile deep. Falstaff's words prompt him into a French drinking song ('Samingo'), often sung in London taverns. Invent actions for Silence in lines 59–61:

'Do me right' – a challenge to drink up

'And dub me knight' – drinkers often knelt to drink in a parody of the ceremony of dubbing a knight

'Samingo', 'Sir Mingo' – the knight of the drinking song ('mingo' is Latin for 'I urinate').

**shrews**  bad-tempered creatures
**Shrovetide**  period of feasting
**mettle**  spirit
**leather-coats**  russet apples
  (with tough skins)
**leman**  sweetheart
**beshrew**  curse me

**cabilleros**  cavaliers, gallants
**crack a quart**  share a drink
**pottle pot**  half gallon tankard
**liggens**  lips (?)
**A will not out**  he won't let
  you down

SILENCE  [*Sings*] Be merry, be merry, my wife has all
          For women are shrews, both short and tall.
          'Tis merry in hall when beards wags all
          And welcome merry Shrovetide, be merry, be merry.    30
FALSTAFF  I did not think Master Silence had been a man of this mettle.
SILENCE  Who, I? I have been merry twice and once ere now.

*Enter* DAVY

DAVY  There's a dish of leather-coats for you.
SHALLOW  Davy!
DAVY  Your worship, I'll be with you straight. – A cup of wine, sir.    35
SILENCE  [*Sings*] A cup of wine, that's brisk and fine,
          And drink unto thee, leman mine,
          And a merry heart lives long-a.
FALSTAFF  Well said, Master Silence.
SILENCE  And we shall be merry, now comes in the sweet a'th'night.    40
FALSTAFF  Health and long life to you, Master Silence.
SILENCE  [*Sings*] Fill the cup, and let it come,
          I'll pledge you a mile to th'bottom.
SHALLOW  Honest Bardolph, welcome. If thou wantest anything and wilt
          not call, beshrew thy heart. – Welcome my little tiny thief, and    45
          welcome indeed too. I'll drink to Master Bardolph, and to all the
          cabilleros about London.
DAVY  I hope to see London once ere I die.
BARDOLPH  And I might see you there, Davy!
SHALLOW  By the Mass, you'll crack a quart together, ha, will you not,    50
          Master Bardolph?
BARDOLPH  Yea, sir, in a pottle pot.
SHALLOW  By God's liggens I thank thee: the knave will stick by thee, I
          can assure thee that. A will not out, a; 'tis true bred.
BARDOLPH  And I'll stick by him, sir.
                                                                        55
SHALLOW  Why, there spoke a king: lack nothing, be merry.

*One knocks at door*

          Look who's at door there, ho; who knocks?
FALSTAFF  Why, now you have done me right.
SILENCE  [*Sings*] Do me right,
          And dub me knight,
                                                                        60
          Samingo.
      Is't not so?

*Pistol brings news from the Court, but his ranting obscures the message for Falstaff who replies in similar bombastic style. Shallow's invitation to speak up or shut up, brings Pistol to the point.*

## 1 Pistol's news (in groups of four or more)

Pistol cannot resist a chance to swagger and bluster. Work out a staging of the final episode from line 67, in which Pistol brings news that Hal is now King Henry V. In your preparation consider:

- Why is Falstaff, normally very quick to catch any meaning, so slow to grasp what Pistol is hinting at?
- Why does Pistol not deliver his news directly?
- How does Pistol speak his six uses of 'and' in lines 75–8?
- Does Silence sing his single line 84 to himself, or in some other way?
- Does Shallow speak lines 90–2 with greatly exaggerated patience and logic, or in some other way?
- 'besonian' (line 93) is a raw recruit. How might Pistol behave to emphasise that he is (or claims to be) an experienced soldier, and Shallow knows nothing of military affairs?
- 'goodman Puff of Barson'. Silence thinks that Pistol's 'greatest man in the realm' refers to Falstaff's size. He claims that the fattest man is goodman (yeoman) Puff of Barson (which may be the village of Barston in Warwickshire). Pistol's response is explosive. He mistakes 'Puff' for 'braggart', and twice insults Silence (lines 74 and 85).

recreant  faith breaker
A foutre  a fig (Elizabethan sexual insult)
worldlings base  ordinary people
Africa  (legendary for wealth)
Assyrian  (Falstaff imitates Pistol's fanciful style)

Cophetua  legendary king who married a beggar maid
Helicons  muses (who in Greek mythology lived on Mount Helicon)
baffled  disgraced
Furies  avenging goddesses

FALSTAFF  'Tis so.

SILENCE  Is't so? Why, then say an old man can do somewhat.

DAVY  And't please your worship, there's one Pistol come from the court  65
with news.

FALSTAFF  From the court? Let him come in.

*Enter* PISTOL

How now, Pistol?

PISTOL  Sir John, God save you.

FALSTAFF  What wind blew you hither, Pistol?  70

PISTOL  Not the ill wind which blows no man to good; sweet knight, thou
art now one of the greatest men in this realm.

SILENCE  By'r Lady, I think a be, but goodman Puff of Barson.

PISTOL  Puff? – Puff i'thy teeth, most recreant coward base!
Sir John, I am thy Pistol and thy friend,  75
And helter-skelter have I rode to thee,
And tidings do I bring, and lucky joys,
And golden times, and happy news of price.

FALSTAFF  I pray thee now, deliver them like a man of this world.

PISTOL  A foutre for the world and worldlings base!  80
I speak of Africa and golden joys.

FALSTAFF  O base Assyrian knight, what is thy news?
Let King Cophetua know the truth thereof.

SILENCE  [*Sings*] And Robin Hood, Scarlet, and John.

PISTOL  Shall dunghill curs confront the Helicons?  85
And shall good news be baffled?
Then Pistol lay thy head in Furies' lap.

SHALLOW  Honest gentleman, I know not your breeding.

PISTOL  Why then, lament therefor.

SHALLOW  Give me pardon, sir. If, sir, you come with news from the  90
court, I take it there's but two ways, either to utter them, or conceal
them. I am, sir, under the king in some authority.

PISTOL  Under which king, besonian? Speak or die.

*Pistol announces his news: King Henry IV is dead, and Hal reigns as Henry V. Falstaff is delighted. He promises rewards for all his friends and punishment for the Lord Chief Justice.*

## 1 The prospect of power (in small groups)

Falstaff thinks that he will become the most powerful man in England now that Hal is king: 'the laws of England are at my commandment'. He feels able to make or break any law, and to do as he pleases: 'Let us take any man's horses'. Think about each of the following as you prepare your staging of this final episode of Scene 3:

a How might an actor speak Falstaff's lines to express his sense of urgency, and his anticipation of the pleasure to come?

b 'Carry Master Silence to bed.' Is Falstaff's command spoken kindly, or dismissively, or …?

c The disorder that has threatened all through the play now seems about to break out in full measure. Falstaff and the others gleefully relish thoughts of the opportunities for exploitation they will enjoy under the new king. Work out a dramatically effective way of staging the bustle and the exits as each man looks forward eagerly to honours, riches and power.

## 2 Dramatic irony

Shakespeare builds in a strong sense of dramatic irony. Falstaff's 'I know the young king is sick for me' and 'woe to my Lord Chief Justice' contrasts ironically with events in the previous scene. Quickly remind yourself of what Prince Hal, now King Henry V, said in the final speech of Scene 2.

---

**fig me** (Pistol makes an obscene gesture with thumb and fingers. It was known as 'the fig of Spain')
**dignities** noble titles
**fortune's steward** manager of patronage (officer who hands out favours)

**Boot** get your riding boots on!
**Let vultures … lungs** in classical mythology, vultures fed on the liver of Titus
**'Where is … led?'** (line from a lost poem or ballad)

SHALLOW  Under King Harry.
PISTOL                    Harry the Fourth, or Fifth?
SHALLOW  Harry the Fourth.
PISTOL                    A foutre for thine office!    95
Sir John, thy tender lambkin now is king:
Harry the Fifth's the man, I speak the truth.
When Pistol lies, do this and fig me, like
The bragging Spaniard.
FALSTAFF                    What, is the old king dead?
PISTOL  As nail in door. The things I speak are just.    100
FALSTAFF  Away, Bardolph, saddle my horse! – Master Robert Shallow,
choose what office thou wilt in the land: 'tis thine. – Pistol, I will
double-charge thee with dignities.
BARDOLPH  O joyful day! I would not take a knighthood for my fortune!
PISTOL  What? I do bring good news.    105
FALSTAFF  Carry Master Silence to bed. Master Shallow, my Lord
Shallow, be what thou wilt: I am fortune's steward. Get on thy
boots, we'll ride all night. O sweet Pistol! Away, Bardolph.

[*Exit Bardolph*]

Come, Pistol, utter more to me, and withal devise something to do
thyself good. – Boot, boot, Master Shallow! I know the young king is    110
sick for me. Let us take any man's horses, the laws of England are at
my commandment. Blessed are they that have been my friends, and
woe to my Lord Chief Justice!
PISTOL  Let vultures vile seize on his lungs also!
'Where is the life that late I led?' say they;    115
Why, here it is: welcome these pleasant days!

*Exeunt*

*The Beadle has arrested Doll and the Hostess for murder and prostitution. They both insult him. Doll claims she is pregnant, but the Beadle says she conceals a cushion beneath her dress.*

The Beadle drags Doll and the Hostess off to prison. In Shakespeare's own company, the Beadle may have been played by John Sincklo, a very thin, pale actor. Pick out all the words and phrases opposite which suggest that the Beadle is skinny and pale.

## 1 Staging the scene (in groups of three)

a  In many productions, Doll has a cushion concealed under her dress to give the impression that she is pregnant, and the Beadle reveals her trick at lines 13–14. But might she really be pregnant? Work out different ways of staging the 'cushion' episode in lines 7–14.

b  Some productions omit this scene. Would you? Consider character, story, theme and dramatic effect. (For example, does the Hostess' comic reversal of 'right' and 'might' in line 20 ironically comment on the political main plot?).

---

**beadle**  parish official
**arrant**  complete
**whipping-cheer**  plenty of whipping (the punishment for prostitutes)
**Nut-hook**  pole with hooked end to gather nuts

**tripe-visaged**  pale and pock-marked
**censer**  perfume dish
**swinged**  beaten
**forswear half-kirtles**  give up wearing skirts
**she-knight-errant**  prostitute
**atomy**  tiny creature

# ACT 5   SCENE 4
## London: the Boar's Head Tavern

Enter HOSTESS QUICKLY, DOLL TEARSHEET and BEADLE

HOSTESS  No, thou arrant knave, I would to God that I might die, that I
might have thee hanged. Thou hast drawn my shoulder out of joint.

BEADLE  The constables have delivered her over to me, and she shall have
whipping-cheer, I warrant her. There hath been a man or two killed
about her.                                                                                    5

DOLL  Nut-hook, nut-hook, you lie. Come on, I'll tell thee what, thou
damned tripe-visaged rascal: and the child I go with do miscarry,
thou wert better thou hadst struck thy mother, thou paper-faced
villain.

HOSTESS  O the Lord, that Sir John were come! I would make this a      10
bloody day to somebody. But I pray God the fruit of her womb
miscarry.

BEADLE  If it do, you shall have a dozen of cushions again: you have but
eleven now. Come, I charge you both go with me, for the man is dead
that you and Pistol beat amongst you.                                              15

DOLL  I'll tell you what, you thin man in a censer: I will have you as
soundly swinged for this, you bluebottle rogue, you filthy famished
correctioner: if you be not swinged, I'll forswear half-kirtles.

BEADLE  Come, come, you she-knight-errant, come.

HOSTESS  O God, that right should thus overcome might! Well, of          20
sufferance comes ease.

DOLL  Come, you rogue, come, bring me to a justice.

HOSTESS  Ay, come, you starved bloodhound.

DOLL  Goodman death, goodman bones.

HOSTESS  Thou atomy, thou.                                                              25

DOLL  Come, you thin thing, come, you rascal.

BEADLE  Very well.

*Exeunt*

*Falstaff and the others line the route to await the king's coronation procession. Falstaff wishes they had better uniforms, but argues that their travel-stained clothes show their devotion.*

## 1 Stage the coronation? (in groups of any size)

The Grooms strew rushes to cover the ceremonial route of the coronation procession. Hal (now King Henry V) enters with all his attendants ('train') and they 'pass over the stage'. On Shakespeare's stage the procession probably entered through one door at the rear of the stage, paraded with great dignity around the stage, and left through another door.

A few productions have staged Hal's coronation ceremony as part of the stage direction at line 4. Work out how you might perform it using all the members of your group.

## 2 Pistol or Shallow?

Pistol repeats Shallow's 'It doth so' at lines 15 and 17. Many productions give all the repetitions to Shallow. Would you? Give a reason for your decision.

## 3 Falstaff's animated speech.

Falstaff's language reveals his excitement and eager anticipation. He is certain that he will be acknowledged by the king, and that his travel-stained clothes will testify to his devotion to the newly-crowned Hal.

Speak Falstaff's lines opposite to express his feeling of confidence and self-importance. Do you think that Falstaff also feels some genuine devotion to Hal?

---

**grooms** male attendants in the king's household
**do you grace** honour you
**leer** smile familiarly

**liveries** uniforms with the king's insignia
**shift me** change my shirt

# ACT 5  SCENE 5
## Near Westminster Abbey

*Enter three* GROOMS *strewing rushes*

FIRST GROOM  More rushes, more rushes!

SECOND GROOM  The trumpets have sounded twice.

THIRD GROOM  'Twill be two a'clock ere they come from the coronation. Dispatch, dispatch!

*Exeunt*

*Trumpets sound and the* KING *and his train pass over the stage. After them enter* FALSTAFF, SHALLOW, PISTOL, BARDOLPH *and the* [PAGE-] BOY

FALSTAFF  Stand here by me, Master Shallow; I will make the king do you grace. I will leer upon him as a comes by, and do but mark the countenance that he will give me.    5

PISTOL  God bless thy lungs, good knight.

FALSTAFF  Come here, Pistol, stand behind me. – O, if I had had time to have made new liveries, I would have bestowed the thousand pound    10
I borrowed of you; but 'tis no matter: this poor show doth better, this doth infer the zeal I had to see him.

SHALLOW  It doth so.

FALSTAFF  It shows my earnestness of affection –

PISTOL  It doth so.    15

FALSTAFF  My devotion –

PISTOL  It doth, it doth, it doth.

FALSTAFF  As it were, to ride day and night, and not to deliberate, not to remember, not to have patience to shift me –

SHALLOW  It is best, certain.    20

FALSTAFF  But to stand stained with travel, and sweating with desire to see him, thinking of nothing else, putting all affairs else in oblivion, as if there were nothing else to be done but to see him.

*Pistol tells Falstaff that Doll has been imprisoned. Falstaff greets King Henry V, who rejects him as a fool and jester who he now despises. He orders Falstaff to reform, and says he himself is a changed man.*

The rejection of Falstaff. In this production, Hal appeared dressed in golden armour, looking like a sun god. Design your own version of the costume worn by the newly crowned king.

## 1 'I know thee not, old man' (in small groups)

How does Hal, now King Henry V, speak his rejection of Falstaff? Use the suggestions below and on page 184 to help you explore different ways of delivering the lines.

- Does Hal pause at some points as he recalls his past friendship?
- Do Hal's words sound like a pompous sermon delivered to the crowd as much as to Falstaff?
- Does he truly mean everything he says? Might Hal be making a joke at lines 49–50?

*semper idem* ever the same
*obsque ... est* apart from this there is nothing
**Helen** beautiful queen (Helen of Troy)
**durance** imprisonment
**contagious** foul

**Haled** dragged
**ebon den** dark cave, hell
**fell Alecto's snake** Alecto was a revenging Fury, with snakes in her hair
**surfeit-swelled** fattened by excess
**gormandising** gluttony, over-eating

PISTOL 'Tis *semper idem*, for *obsque hoc nihil est*; 'tis all in every part.
SHALLOW 'Tis so, indeed.                                                    25
PISTOL My knight, I will inflame thy noble liver,
    And make thee rage.
    Thy Doll, and Helen of thy noble thoughts,
    Is in base durance and contagious prison,
    Haled thither                                            30
    By most mechanical and dirty hands.
    Rouse up Revenge from ebon den with fell Alecto's snake,
    For Doll is in. Pistol speaks nought but truth.
FALSTAFF I will deliver her.

*The trumpets sound*

PISTOL There roared the sea, and trumpet clangour sounds.              35

*Enter the* KING *and his train*

FALSTAFF God save thy grace, King Hal, my royal Hal.
PISTOL The heavens thee guard and keep,
    Most royal imp of fame.
FALSTAFF God save thee, my sweet boy.
KING My Lord Chief Justice, speak to that vain man.                    40
JUSTICE Have you your wits? Know you what 'tis you speak?
FALSTAFF My king, my Jove, I speak to thee, my heart.
KING I know thee not, old man. Fall to thy prayers.
    How ill white hairs becomes a fool and jester!
    I have long dreamt of such a kind of man,                  45
    So surfeit-swelled, so old and so profane,
    But being awaked, I do despise my dream.
    Make less thy body hence, and more thy grace,
    Leave gormandising, know the grave doth gape
    For thee thrice wider than for other men.                  50
    Reply not to me with a fool-born jest,
    Presume not that I am the thing I was,
    For God doth know – so shall the world perceive –
    That I have turned away my former self;
    So will I those that kept me company.                      55
    When thou dost hear I am as I have been,
    Approach me, and thou shalt be as thou wast,
    The tutor and the feeder of my riots;

*The king banishes Falstaff, granting him a pension, and promising promotion if he reforms. Falstaff denies Shallow his thousand pounds, saying the king will send for him. He is arrested and sent to prison.*

## 1 The rejection of Falstaff (use also with page 182)

a Advise the actor playing Falstaff how to react as King Henry speaks his lines of rejection (for example, is he dumbstruck? does he attempt to protest? does he think it one of Hal's jokes?, and so on).

b Give your response to the claim that the rejection episode symbolises each of the following themes:
• the restoration of order after disorder
• the triumph of political expediency ('policy')
• the inevitable changes brought about by time
• evidence of corruption in human and social life.

c Does Falstaff get what he deserves? Give your personal reaction to the way in which Hal rejects Falstaff, and to Falstaff's arrest and imprisonment.

d What final impression would you wish the audience to form? That Falstaff is utterly humiliated and panic-stricken? or optimistic, proud and in control? or …?

## 2 Falstaff and Shallow (in pairs)

Falstaff has borrowed £1000 from Justice Shallow, who now wants it repaid. It was a vast sum, £1 could buy you 240 loaves of bread.

Play lines 69–83 several times, taking turns as Falstaff and Shallow. How does Falstaff speak to Shallow: jokingly, sadly, coldly, shamefacedly, businesslike, or …? What is Shallow's tone? When Falstaff says he will be sent for by Hal, does he really believe it?

---

**competence of life** necessary expenses
**tenor** substance
**advancements** future promotions
**colour** pretence (line 80), hangman's noose (line 81), enemy banners (line 82)

**Fleet** prison
*Se fortuna* … if fortune torments me, hope contents me
**intent** ordered
**wonted** former

Till then I banish thee, on pain of death,
As I have done the rest of my misleaders,                           60
Not to come near our person by ten mile.
For competence of life I will allow you,
That lack of means enforce you not to evils;
And as we hear you do reform yourselves,
We will, according to your strengths and qualities,               65
Give you advancement. – Be it your charge, my lord,
To see performed the tenor of my word.
Set on.                                                  *Exit King [and train]*

FALSTAFF Master Shallow, I owe you a thousand pound.

SHALLOW Yea, marry, Sir John, which I beseech you to let me have home   70
with me.

FALSTAFF That can hardly be, Master Shallow. Do not you grieve at this.
I shall be sent for in private to him. Look you, he must seem thus to
the world. Fear not your advancements: I will be the man yet that
shall make you great.                                                 75

SHALLOW I cannot perceive how, unless you give me your doublet and
stuff me out with straw. I beseech you, good Sir John, let me have
five hundred of my thousand.

FALSTAFF Sir, I will be as good as my word. This that you heard was but
a colour.                                                             80

SHALLOW A colour that I fear you will die in, Sir John.

FALSTAFF Fear no colours, go with me to dinner. Come, Lieutenant
Pistol, come, Bardolph. I shall be sent for soon at night.

*Enter the* LORD CHIEF JUSTICE *and Prince* JOHN, *[with Officers]*

JUSTICE Go, carry Sir John Falstaff to the Fleet,
Take all his company along with him.                                  85

FALSTAFF My lord, my lord –

JUSTICE I cannot now speak, I will hear you soon.
Take them away.

PISTOL *Se fortuna mi tormenta, ben sperato mi contenta –*

*Exeunt [all but Prince John and Lord Chief Justice]*

JOHN I like this fair proceeding of the king's:                       90
He hath intent his wonted followers
Shall all be very well provided for,
But all are banished till their conversations
Appear more wise and modest to the world.

*Prince John forecasts that an English army will soon invade France. The Epilogue apologises for a previous play, reports that Falstaff will appear in a further play, and claims that Falstaff is not Oldcastle.*

## 1 Shakespeare's next play? (in pairs)

Prince John's speech shows that Hal has taken his father's advice to 'busy giddy minds with foreign quarrels'. It looks forward to *Henry V* in which the king leads an English army to France, and wins a famous victory at Agincourt.

Many actors consider this a very downbeat way to end the play. Do you agree? Make your own suggestion of how you would play lines 90–102.

## 2 The Epilogue

The Epilogue is mainly about some theatrical event, now long forgotten. It has three sections, and in Shakespeare's time, probably only one of the three sections would be spoken.

Lines 1–14 apologise for a play that did not please the audience. No one today knows the name of the 'displeasing play'. The section ends with an invitation to pray for the Queen.

Lines 15–21 are a promise by the actor to dance in recompense for the displeasing play.

Lines 22–8 promise that Falstaff will be seen in a future play (*Henry V* ), and asserts that Falstaff is not Oldcastle (see page 197). This section also ends in a dance. (Falstaff does not appear in *Henry V*, but his death is movingly reported by the Hostess.)

Who speaks the Epilogue? Some suggestions have been: Shakespeare himself for Section 1; the Page for Section 2; and a dancer for Section 3.

Many modern productions cut the Epilogue altogether. Suggest what you would do if you were directing the play.

---

**parliament** see page 171, lines 140–1
**lay odds** bet
**civil swords ... fire** army and courage
**curtsy** bow
**marring** spoiling, damaging

**ill venture** unsuccessful trading voyage
**bate me some** let me off part of my debt
**cloyed** surfeited, overfull
**sweat** fever or sexually transmitted disease

JUSTICE  And so they are.                                                    95
JOHN  The king hath called his parliament, my lord.
JUSTICE  He hath.
JOHN  I will lay odds that, ere this year expire,
    We bear our civil swords and native fire
    As far as France. I heard a bird so sing,                      100
    Whose music, to my thinking, pleased the king.
    Come, will you hence?

*Exeunt*

## EPILOGUE

First my fear, then my curtsy, last my speech.

My fear is your displeasure, my curtsy my duty, and my speech
to beg your pardons. If you look for a good speech now, you undo
me, for what I have to say is of mine own making; and what indeed
I should say will, I doubt, prove mine own marring. But to the          5
purpose, and so to the venture. Be it known to you, as it is very well,
I was lately here in the end of a displeasing play, to pray your
patience for it and to promise you a better. I meant indeed to pay
you with this, which, if like an ill venture it come unluckily home,
I break, and you, my gentle creditors, lose. Here I promised you I      10
would be, and here I commit my body to your mercies: bate me
some, and I will pay you some, and, as most debtors do, promise
infinitely. And so I kneel down before you, but, indeed, to pray for
the queen.

If my tongue cannot entreat you to acquit me, will you command          15
me to use my legs? And yet that were but light payment, to dance
out of your debt. But a good conscience will make any possible
satisfaction, and so would I. All the gentlewomen here have
forgiven me; if the gentlemen will not, then the gentlemen do not
agree with the gentlewomen, which was never seen in such an             20
assembly.

One word more, I beseech you: if you be not too much cloyed
with fat meat, our humble author will continue the story with Sir
John in it, and make you merry with fair Katherine of France,
where, for anything I know, Falstaff shall die of a sweat, unless       25
already a be killed with your hard opinions; for Oldcastle died
martyr, and this is not the man. My tongue is weary; when my legs
are too, I will bid you good night.

# Looking back at the play
*Activities for groups or individuals*

## 1 How would you end the play?

All performances aim to end the play with a memorable stage picture. Work out the final image the audience sees in your own production.

## 2 Dramatic construction

Turn back to Activity 6 on page 39 and remind yourself of how Shakespeare structures the play to ensure that each scene contains ironic and dramatic contrasts with its neighbouring scenes. Then select two or three scenes and suggest how the comic subplot mirrors or inverts the main political plot. Consider characters, action, and such themes as order and disorder, England, sickness and disease, and so on.

## 3 Women in a man's world

a You have been invited to write a paragraph entitled 'Women in a man's world' for a theatre programme for *Part 2*. Write your paragraph.

b Step into role as a feminist director of the play. Suggest some major features of your production. Begin by considering whether the play appeals differently to males and females.

## 4 An unpleasant play?

The tone or atmosphere of the play has sometimes been described as unpleasant and disturbing, lacking love or pity. List some reasons why you think those descriptions have been used, then give your own judgement about the prevailing mood of the play.

## 5 One play or two?

*Henry IV Part 2* was probably written around 1597–8. It may have been written as a sequel to exploit the great success of *Part 1*. Or perhaps Shakespeare had started out to write one play on the reign of Henry IV but found he had too much material, so split it into two plays. When you have read both plays, give your own view on whether or not Shakespeare originally intended to write two separate plays.

## 6 'A man or two killed'

The Beadle arresting the Hostess says that she and Pistol murdered a man in her tavern. What lies behind the Beadle's accusation? Write a newspaper report of what happened, linking your story to themes and characters in the play.

## 7 A lesson in politics?

What do you learn about politics from the play? Prepare a presentation of some kind (for example, an essay, or a dramatic presentation) to show how the play illustrates political practices and issues today.

## 8 Cameo roles

*Part 2* is popular with students because there are many cameo roles: Shallow, Silence, the Hostess, Doll, Falstaff's recruits, Fang, and so on. Choose one such character, and work out how you would play him or her.

## 9 Gloucestershire: a model community?

What is Shakespeare's own attitude to life in rural England as he portrays it in the Gloucestershire scenes? Mocking? Gently affectionate and respectful? Admiring its sense of community? Or ...?

## 10 Design opportunities

Choose one or more of the following design tasks: costumes for two or three characters; a coat of arms for Falstaff; campaign medals for the defeat of the rebellion; a programme cover or poster advertising the play.

## 11 Putting the audience in the picture

What knowledge of history does an audience need? Write a programme note that you feel will help an audience who are seeing *Part 2* for the very first time.

## 12 What happened to Falstaff?

In Robert Nye's novel *Falstaff* (1976), the fat knight does not die when Shakespeare killed him off in *Henry V*, but lives on to a great age. He sees the battle of Agincourt and the capture of Joan of Arc. Step into role as Falstaff and invent your story of what happens to you after the end of *Part 2*.

# What is the play about?

As always in Shakespeare, there is no single answer to the question 'What is the play about?' One approach is to tell the story, for example by reading the summaries of the action at the top of each left-hand page. You might even try to sum up the story in a single sentence: 'This history play shows how the unsuccessful rebellion by the Archbishop of York against King Henry is mirrored by the comic sub-plot in which Prince Hal finally rejects Falstaff'.

Another approach is to see *Henry IV Part 2* as Shakespeare's re-working of medieval morality plays in which a symbolic character, Vice, tries to tempt a young man into disorderly behaviour. At the end of such plays, Vice is banished into Hell, and the young man is redeemed to goodness. Falstaff represents the tempter, determined to profit from his corruption of Prince Hal, the young man.

The play is Shakespeare's dramatic version of the period 1403–13. The Falstaff episodes echo and ironically comment on the main plot of political rebellion and double dealing. Viewed in this way, the play can be seen as a satire on the morality of politics and justice. The relationships of the main plot and the comic sub-plot can be understood by considering some of the major themes of the play.

## Time – 'We are Time's subjects'

A strong sense of time pervades the play, but in very different ways. The rebels plan for the future, just as King Henry hopes to lead a crusade to the Holy Land when the rebellion is crushed. In contrast, in the tavern, Falstaff is determined to ignore time, living for the pleasures of the moment.

Perhaps the strongest sense of time is of the past, and of the inevitability of death. The king and the rebels look back with unease or anger to the events that brought Henry to the throne: the deposition and murder of Richard II. In the tavern, Falstaff begs Doll not to remind him of his death. In Gloucestershire, Shallow, Silence and Falstaff recall dead friends and their student days, fifty-five years ago. These scenes are often played on stage to create a mood of autumnal melancholy evoked by such lines as Falstaff's 'We have heard the chimes at midnight' and Shallow's 'All shall die'.

# Order and disorder – 'O my poor kingdom!'

Throughout the play, England is threatened with collapse into the chaos of disorder. King Henry, having defeated Hotspur's rebellion (in *Part 1*), faces renewed rebellion led by the Archbishop. In the very first scene, the rebel Northumberland declares the theme with chilling directness: 'let Order die.'

Many in Shakespeare's own audience would recognise Northumberland's words as an expression of what has become known as 'the Tudor Myth'. This was a view of history that saw Henry Bullingbrook's deposition of King Richard II as an offence against God. God's punishment was the rebellions during Henry's reign and the subsequent disorders of the Wars of the Roses, ended only when the first Tudor king, Henry VII, defeated Richard III and restored order to England.

The argument goes that Elizabethans believed in 'the Great Chain of Being': a natural order in nature and society. According to this view (sometimes called the Elizabethan World Picture), God sat at the top of a hierarchy, with angels below him, men and women below them and so on down to the smallest creatures and to inanimate matter.

This hierarchical view appealed especially to monarchs, who claimed themselves to be God's representatives on earth. They asserted that any rebellion against a king was a rebellion against God. In churches, schools, history books and official proclamations, the message was preached that the existing hierarchical order was good, and that any challenge to that order was bad. For example, the Homily on Disobedience was read four times each year in every church in England (and at the time every citizen was compelled to attend church).

Shakespeare deepens the theme of disorder in the comic sub-plot. He pits Falstaff, who threatens to bring about anarchy, against the Lord Chief Justice, who stands for law and order. Just as the rebels threaten political chaos, so Falstaff represents the overthrow of authority. Henry fears that when Hal (who he believes is abandoned to riot and disorder) becomes king, all the high offices of state will be given to Hal's debauched followers: 'apes of idleness', who 'swear, drink, dance, Revel the night, rob, murder …'.

Falstaff, hearing that his beloved Prince Hal has become king, thinks he can now satisfy all his desires: 'The laws of England are at my commandment. Blessed are they that have been my friends, and woe to my Lord Chief Justice!' But the play appears to end with order restored: Falstaff is banished, and the rebels have been executed.

## Sickness and disease – 'We are all diseased'

The play is full of images of disease and corruption. Northumberland is first heard of as being 'crafty-sick', and Falstaff jokes about his own ill health 'A pox of this gout, or a gout of this pox'. King Henry appears on his sickbed, ill in body and mind.

The king's reflection on the rank diseases that grow in 'the body of our kingdom' acknowledges the political and spiritual corruption of the land at every social level from top to bottom. The Archbishop leads a rebellion: a 'fearful war' to purge the sickness of the state. In the Boar's Head Tavern, Doll Tearsheet spreads sexual diseases. Falstaff's corruption is exposed in the recruiting scene. Hearing of Hal's accession to the throne, he hopes for power under the new king, and threatens to bring chaos to England.

## Policy – 'A good wit will make use of anything'

'Policy' can be described in all kinds of ways: heartlessness, hypocrisy, treachery, machiavellianism, deception, expediency, realpolitik. All are the opposite of trust and integrity.

When Falstaff, old and sick, sees personal advantage in his condition ('I will turn diseases to commodity'), his joking remark symbolises this major theme of the play. Many characters are willing to use any means to achieve their ends. Falstaff exploits the Hostess and Shallow. He intends to use Hal to achieve even greater gains. Shallow hopes to use Falstaff to gain influence at court.

In the main plot, 'policy' results in treachery and betrayal. In Gaultree Forest, Prince John tricks the rebels into believing his promises are sincere and honourable. King Henry plans a crusade. It may seem like the duty of a Christian king, but it is partly to assuage his troubled conscience, and even more to prevent his subjects having time to think about his questionable right to be king of England. Henry advises Hal to use the same machiavellian expediency, and 'busy giddy minds with foreign quarrels'.

In Act 4 Scene 2, lines 68–78, Warwick recognises Hal's manipulation of the tavern set: the prince will in time cast off his disorderly friends, because he is only using them to find out what kinds of people he will rule over. That rejection comes in the final scene with the banishment of Falstaff.

# England

Many people claim that England is the true subject and hero of *Part 2*. Its recurring presence throughout the play takes many different forms, most obviously in the names of places and people.

In alternating scenes the action ranges across England, from Northumberland's Warkworth castle to the king's court or Hostess Quickly's tavern in London; from the rural tranquillity of Justice Shallow's orchard in Gloucestershire to the sombre setting of Gaultree Forest in Yorkshire, scene of Prince John's treacherous entrapment of the rebels.

London is vividly portrayed. Hostess Quickly conjures up the bustle of the city as she tells that Falstaff 'comes continuantly to Pie Corner – saving your manhoods – to buy a saddle, and he is indited to dinner to the Lubber's Head in Lumbert Street to Master Smooth's the silkman'. Justice Shallow recalls his youthful exploits at Clement's Inn, Mile End Green (where he played King Arthur's fool, Sir Dagonet, in a pageant), and in the windmill in Saint George's Field.

The countryside also takes on a physical presence as people and places are memorably associated: William Visor of Woncot, Clement Perkes a'th'Hill, little John Doit of Staffordshire, Will Squele, a Cotswold man, Goodman Puff of Barson. Falstaff uses a very English joke to insult Poins: 'his wit's as thick as Tewkesbury mustard'. The world of Gloucestershire farming springs to life in the language: hade land, red wheat, pigeons, shoeing, plough-irons, links and buckets, Hinckley Fair, muttons and short-legged hens.

Moving between palace and people, the play evokes a complex social and symbolic impression of England. But the corruption and decay evident in both main and sub-plot create an atmosphere unlike the conventional image of 'Merrie England'. The rebels threaten to destroy national unity, and King Henry's and Falstaff's bodily sickness is reflected in the diseased state of England itself. Both Henry and Falstaff look forward, with very different feelings, to the anarchy that will prevail when Hal becomes king of England.

The England of the play is very selective in its presentation of women. Lady Northumberland and Lady Percy make only one appearance and clearly lack power. Similarly lacking in power, Hostess Quickly is an exploited innkeeper, and Doll Tearsheet a foul-mouthed prostitute. They have been compared with Falstaff's recruits: working-class people pressed unwillingly into service to serve the purposes of the king – and to fill Falstaff's pockets.

## Necessity – 'the rough torrent of occasion'

A modern British prime minister was asked what was the most difficult aspect of government. His reply was 'Events'. Shakespeare's play dramatises the same political need to respond to unexpected happenings.

The Archbishop calls the events that have caused his rebellion 'the rough torrent of occasion'. Henry talks of 'chance's mocks and changes', and, prompted by Warwick, sees them as 'necessities' that must be met with strong action. Westmoreland urges Mowbray to 'Construe the times to their necessities', urging him to recognise the practicalities that have caused the rebels' grievances.

In the comic sub-plot, Falstaff erupts into Shallow's tranquil world with disastrous results for the Gloucestershire Justice. A similar unexpected event frustrates Falstaff's plans and expectations: Prince Hal does not turn out to be a friend after all.

## Appearance and reality – 'Let's drink together, friendly'

The opening speech of the play declares that things will not be what they seem. Rumour speaks of 'false reports' and 'comforts false'. As in every Shakespeare play, reality does not conform with appearance, and *Part 2* contains all kinds of miscalculations and failures of perception.

King Henry, the Lord Chief Justice and Falstaff all misjudge Prince Hal, thinking him wild and riotous, lacking the qualities to be a good king. Shallow and the Hostess mistake the corrupt Falstaff for a trustworthy gentleman. The Archbishop and his fellow rebels fatally fail to recognise Prince John's true nature. Henry may have the appearance of a king, but he knows that in reality his title to the crown is weak.

a Other themes include: fathers and sons (real and symbolic – both Falstaff and the Lord Chief Justice are substitute fathers to Hal); debts and obligations (every character 'owes' something to other characters, most obviously Falstaff's debt of £1000 to Shallow); the education of a prince (the choices Hal must make between Falstaff's world and the world of royal duty, see page 195). Identify characters, incidents and lines to show how each theme occurs in the play.

b Design a stage prop which acts as a constant reminder of some major theme of the play (for example, one production had a large map of England as a permanent backdrop throughout the performance).

# Characters

## Prince Hal – 'The prince but studies his companions'

There is a long tradition that portrays each Prince of Wales as a loose-living free spirit. Prince Hal is perhaps the best-known example of that tradition. In *Part 1*, he joins in a robbery, enjoys a close personal relationship with the corrupt Falstaff, and is called a madcap. In *Part 2*, there are mentions of his being sent to prison for boxing the ears of the Lord Chief Justice. His father, King Henry, despairs of his 'headstrong riot', fearing that when Hal is king, England will become 'a wilderness again, Peopled with wolves'.

But Henry, like Falstaff, is mistaken about Hal's character. Both see Hal as wild and dissolute, living only for pleasure. Warwick is more perceptive. He says that Hal 'but studies his companions' and will 'in the perfectness of time Cast off his followers' (Act 4 Scene 2, lines 68–78). Warwick's words echo Hal's soliloquy in *Part 1*, where, at the end of the first tavern scene, he reveals that his riotous behaviour is merely a pretence.

One interpretation of *Part 2* claims it is about 'the education of a prince' (especially when it is played in a cycle with *Part 1* and *Henry V*). The play is seen as Hal's 'growing up', his search for identity as he is faced with choice of role model: Falstaff or King Henry? This approach focuses on the development of Hal's character as he makes his choice between idleness and the hard work of royal duty, between the tavern and the court.

Like the prodigal son in the Bible, Hal recovers the reputation he has lost. As *Part 2* draws to its close, he is reconciled with his father, declares himself for law and order, and rejects Falstaff. His waste of time in foolery and horseplay in the tavern is seen as a rite of passage, the ritual through which he is transformed from adolescent to adult.

Hal does not appear to be much of a madcap in *Part 2*. His only escapade is disguising himself as a potboy to spy on Falstaff. On his first appearance, Hal seems full of self-disgust for idling away his time and 'keeping such vile company'. He becomes increasingly serious in each appearance, and shares only two scenes with Falstaff: first in the Boar's Head Tavern; second in the final scene, where, as King Henry V, he banishes the fat knight.

- What is your view of Hal's character? Is he hypocritical and heartless in rejecting Falstaff? Or is he sincere, genuinely loving his father, and enjoying the friendship he finds in the tavern? Or ...?

## Falstaff – 'The tutor and the feeder of my riots'

In spite of his very obvious faults, Falstaff has been a hugely popular character on stage for four hundred years. In *Part 2*, he is often judged to be less humorous and less likeable than in *Part 1*. He appears unscrupulous and malicious as he preys on Justice Shallow and Hostess Quickly, exploiting the friendship and hospitality that both offer him. Contemptuous of law and justice, he looks forward to revenging himself on his main adversary: 'Woe to my Lord Chief Justice!'

Similar evaluations have been made of Falstaff in both *Parts 1* and *2*: thief, liar, parasite, drunkard, lecher, braggart, swindler, fraud, sponger and glutton. Seeing the prospect of power under the new king, he orders 'take any man's horses, the laws of England are at my commandment'. Always an opportunist, and ready to exploit others for his own advantage, he makes use of anything that will serve his interests. When he thinks that his gout (or pox) will make him limp, he decides to pretend the limp is a war wound, saying 'A good wit will make use of anything. I will turn diseases to commodity.'

Falstaff's youthful experience as a page to the Duke of Norfolk and as a student at Clement's Inn have given him a good education. In *Part 2*, he may seem obsessed by his social rank and fame as a war hero, but his language shows evidence of his learning, full of images drawn from the Bible, medicine, history, literature, logic and music.

Falstaff's dramatic function in the play has been described as:

*Scapegoat*: Falstaff is rejected and driven out, taking with him the stain and dishonour of Hal's riotous youth.

*Substitute father*: in opposition to Hal's cold, stern father.

*Teacher*: helping Hal to learn about the people of England.

*Vice*: who, in medieval morality plays, tried unsuccessfully to corrupt young men. At the end of the play, he is banished into Hell.

*'Holy Fool'*: subverting authority and traditional values.

*Lord of Misrule*: a grotesque figure with a giant appetite for food, drink, sex and riot, who, in medieval festivals, ruled only for a short period.

The Epilogue at the end of the play closes with 'Oldcastle died martyr, and this is not the man'. In the first performances of the play, Falstaff was originally called Oldcastle. Shakespeare changed the name, probably because of protests from Oldcastle's descendants who held high office under Queen Elizabeth I. They objected to seeing their famous ancestor scandalously misrepresented and made into a figure of fun on stage.

Sir John Oldcastle was a famous Protestant hero and martyr. As a young man he had been a friend of Prince Hal, for whom he fought bravely in France. Oldcastle became a Lollard, a member of a Protestant movement that challenged England's dominant Catholic orthodoxy. The Lollards were labelled as heretics who blasphemed against the 'true' religion. The punishment for heresy was death, and for his beliefs, Oldcastle was burnt at the stake on Christmas Day 1417, aged only 39.

Falstaff has inspired all kinds of re-creations: in opera and music, novels and films, paintings, sculptures, tavern signs – and even on beer mats. How close is this statue to your own image of Falstaff?

## King Henry – 'Uneasy lies the head that wears a crown'

Although the play is named after him, King Henry is hardly its hero. He does not appear until Act 3 Scene 1 where he is shown unable to sleep, a sure sign to Elizabethan audiences of a troubled conscience. He feels guilt for the overthrow and murder of King Richard II, and he knows that his own right to be king is weak, because he gained the crown through 'by-paths and indirect crooked ways'.

Henry appears old and ill, mirroring the decay and sickness of England itself. He wishes to leave a united kingdom and a secure, legitimate title to his eldest son, Prince Hal. But he faces a rebellion led by the Archbishop, and he fears that after his death, Hal's wildness will cause England to collapse into anarchy.

Henry plans his crusade to Jerusalem to serve two purposes. It will excuse his sin in seizing the crown, and it will fully occupy his rebellious nobles, preventing them from questioning his right to rule. He advises Hal to use the same tactic when he becomes king, and 'busy giddy minds with foreign quarrels'.

## Other characters

Use the following brief descriptions as starting points for your investigation of a chosen character (for example, their motives, how other characters view them, their version of the story, and so on).

*Lord Chief Justice*: The main opponent of Falstaff. He is the play's symbol of integrity and justice. (Is that why Shakespeare gave him no personal name?) Might he secretly like Falstaff?

*Hostess*: Much exploited by Falstaff, and the butt of his jokes. Kind-hearted and credulous, she loves language but misuses words.

*Pistol*: A braggart, fraudulent soldier (the *miles gloriosus* of Italian comedies, a coward who pretends to be brave). He swaggers and boasts, and uses exaggerated language full of misquotations.

*Doll Tearsheet*: A quarrelsome, foul-mouthed prostitute. Is she Shakespeare's parody of romantic love?

*Shallow*: Garrulous, vain and ambitious, he wants influence at court. Is his playing Dagonet (a fool) in his youth the key to his character?

*Prince John*: Machiavellian in his deceit in Gaultree Forest. Cold and unsympathetic. Is he the only effective leader in the play?

*Northumberland*: Cautious and rational. He fails to deliver his promised support for the Archbishop's rebellion. Why?

*Poins*: Seems very close to Prince Hal, but disappears from the play after Act 2. Is he high or low social class?

# The language of the play

## Verse and prose

Shakespeare's theatre audiences generally expected to hear high-status characters using verse, and prose used for comedy or by low-status characters. So whilst the Falstaff scenes ('comic') are in prose, the court and rebel scenes ('serious', with high-status characters) are mainly in blank verse (unrhymed verse). Each ten-syllable line of blank verse has five alternating unstressed (x) and stressed (/) syllables (iambic pentameter), as in King Henry's:

```
x  /  x   /  x   /   x   /  x   /
Uneasy lies the head that wears a crown
```

But Shakespeare did not follow any stage convention slavishly, and used verse or prose appropriate to the mood and nature of a scene, 'serious' or 'comic'. Prince Hal and the Lord Chief Justice have very high status, but both use prose in the company of Falstaff. When Hal, as King Henry V, rejects Falstaff, he uses verse to signify the seriousness of the moment: 'I know thee not, old man. Fall to thy prayers.'

## Imagery (metaphor, simile, personification)

Imagery is the use of vivid words and phrases which conjure up emotionally charged pictures in the imagination. When Falstaff first appears followed by his Page, he claims he is 'like a sow that hath overwhelmed all her litter but one'.

All Shakespeare's imagery uses metaphor or simile. Both are comparisons: a simile uses 'like' or 'as' in the comparison, a metaphor does not. When King Henry calls sleep 'Nature's soft nurse' he uses a metaphor to describe the healing power of sleep. But when Hastings pictures the king's army as 'like a fangless lion', he uses a simile.

Personification turns things or ideas into human beings, giving them human feelings or body parts. There are many personifications in the play: Rumour, War, Jealousy, Death, Time, Spite, Order, Nature, Rebellion, Sleep, Fame, Revenge, Justice, Sickness, Vanity.

- Turn to two pages at random and identify as many images as you can. Find a way of enacting or displaying each image (for example as a tableau or as a poster).

## Lists

One of Shakespeare's favourite methods with language was to accumulate words or phrases rather like a list. He knew that 'piling up' item on item, incident on incident, can intensify description, atmosphere, argument and dramatic effect.

Some lists are long, for example Falstaff's description of the effects of drinking sack (Act 4 Scene 1, lines 431–48), and the Lord Chief Justice's description of Falstaff in Act 1 Scene 2:

> 'Have you not a moist eye, a dry hand, a yellow cheek, a white beard, a decreasing leg, an increasing belly? Is not your voice broken, your wind short, your chin double, your wit single, and every part about you blasted with antiquity?'

Other lists are short but just as revealing of character or theme, for example in Doll's description of the Beadle who arrests her (Act 5 Scene 4, lines 6–9): 'Nut-hook', 'damned tripe-visaged rascal', 'paper-faced villain'.

- Turn at random to three or four pages of the script. On every page you will find a list of some kind. Suggest what kind of list it is, what function it fulfils in the play. Speak each list in a style you think suitable. Some of your lists will lend themselves to acting out.

## Language is character

Shakespeare gives each character his or her own distinctive language, appropriate to the speaker's meaning, mood and situation. King Henry reveals his troubled conscience in the questioning tone of his soliloquy on sleep, but becomes brisk and businesslike in his determination to overcome the rebels:

> Are these things then necessities?
> Then let us meet them like necessities.

The eccentric personalities of the comic characters are strikingly created by their language:

> Justice Shallow, who so often exaggerates his memories of his youthful exploits, has a matching language characteristic: repetition. It is evident in the very first words he speaks: 'Come on, come on, come on, sir, give me your hand, sir, give me your hand, sir.'

Hostess Quickly tells long rambling stories. Her fondness for high-sounding words results in malapropisms, 'honeysuckle' for 'homicidal', 'infinitive' for 'infinite', and so on.

Pistol's language is bombastic: his explosive verbal excess full of sound and fury signifying very little. He prefers sound to sense in his mixture of bragging, boasting and half-remembered quotations from old plays.

Doll Tearsheet, the streetwise prostitute, has tender moments with Falstaff, but her language is mostly shrill and colourful abuse as she insults Pistol and the Beadle who arrests her.

Falstaff's language in *Part 1* was dazzlingly various and inventive, filled with imaginative energy. He lied, boasted, insulted, punned, ridiculed, and talked exaggerated nonsense. In *Part 2*, the same characteristics are present in his language, and he continues to employ many extravagant images. But because he seems more concerned with age and disease, his tone seems more serious, less joyous.

He still insults others, often slyly or in soliloquy behind other characters' backs. He cleverly uses language to get himself out of trouble, to evade giving direct answers, to exploit others, twist meanings and inflate his status, power and wealth. The Lord Chief Justice accurately describes Falstaff's language style as 'impudent sauciness', and 'the manner of wrenching the true cause the false way'.

## Names

The names of many of the characters gives a clue to their personality. Pistol is like an Elizabethan hand gun: explosive, unpredictable, liable to go off at any moment with a deafening, incomprehensible bang.

But Shakespeare was too skilled a dramatist to put simple stereotypes on stage, mere one-dimensional caricatures. He provides clues to characters' personalities in their names, but gives them language which allows actors to create real human beings, full of contradictions. Bullcalf turns out to be a coward, and Feeble, the woman's tailor, shows soldier-like courage: 'a man can die but once'.

# History into drama

In *Henry IV Part 2*, Shakespeare dramatises events between 1403 and 1413: from shortly after the battle of Shrewsbury to the death of King Henry IV and the crowning of Prince Hal as King Henry V.

All kinds of material fired Shakespeare's dramatic imagination: folk tales about the wildness of Prince Hal before he became king; popular chronicle plays (for example, *The Famous Victories of Henry the Fifth*, with an unruly Prince Hal and the disreputable Jockey Oldcastle); and medieval morality plays in which a young man was tempted into mischief by Vice, but redeemed by Virtue (corresponding to Hal, Falstaff and the Lord Chief Justice).

Shakespeare's major source was *Holinshed's Chronicles of England, Scotland and Ireland* (1587). It presented history from the viewpoint of the Tudor dynasty, portraying the civil wars of the fifteenth century as God's punishment for Henry IV's unlawful seizure of the crown.

Shakespeare wrote his own version of history to suit his dramatic purposes. Unlike Holinshed, he gives Prince John the leading role in the betrayal in Gaultree Forest. He makes the play's events seem to flow in quick succession. In reality, the battle of Shewsbury was fought in 1403, the Archbishop rebelled and was executed in 1405, Northumberland and Bardolph were defeated in 1408, Glendower died in 1409, and Henry became very ill in 1412 and died in 1413.

*Part 2* embodies the political, social and personal preoccupations of Shakespeare's own time. The Rebellion of the North in 1569 against Queen Elizabeth I was still fearfully remembered, and there was anxiety about who should succeed the queen. That apprehension is reflected in a question that lies at the heart of the play: 'Who is the rightful monarch?'

But Shakespeare's major sources were his imagination, his love of language and his own conception of England. His creation of Falstaff shows him at his most inventive, bringing to life a superb comic character, and making the fat knight's scenes provide ironic parallels and contrasts to the political plot.

- Step into role as Shakespeare. Tell why you have written the play, why you have produced your own version of history, and why you have invented Falstaff, Shallow and the other 'comic' characters.

# Staging the play

Falstaff and his comic companions have proved immensely popular figures since they first stepped on stage in the late 1590s. Adaptations long after Shakespeare's death exploited their appeal (for example, *Falstaff's Wedding* of 1760). In the eighteenth and nineteenth centuries, productions emphasised historical costumes, sets and ceremonies. Magnificent scenes of Prince Hal's coronation as King Henry V were added, and one production included 'A Grand Musical Festival'.

The twentieth century has seen major changes in staging and interpretation. The Gloucestershire scenes are usually played in a mood of nostalgic and elegiac melancholy, emphasising the theme of time and decay. *Part 2* is often paired with *Part 1*, or is performed in a cycle of history plays (see page 1) to show Shakespeare's story of the working out of the consequences of Henry's wrongful seizure of the throne of England. Such stagings highlight power politics, and how the Falstaff scenes parallel and ironically comment on the serious plot.

The play has almost always been performed in Elizabethan or medieval costumes and settings. This Royal Shakespeare Company staging used metal-clad walls and floors for the whole cycle of history plays.
The set shown is for Act 3 Scene 1: King Henry's room (in *Part 2*).
What impression of the play do you think the set designer wished to create?

# William Shakespeare 1564–1616

1564 Born Stratford-upon-Avon, eldest son of John and Mary Shakespeare.
1582 Marries Anne Hathaway of Shottery, near Stratford.
1583 Daughter, Susanna, born.
1585 Twins, son and daughter, Hamnet and Judith, born.
1592 First mention of Shakespeare in London. Robert Greene, another playwright, described Shakespeare as 'an upstart crow beautified with our feathers ...'. Greene seems to have been jealous of Shakespeare. He mocked Shakespeare's name, calling him 'the only Shake-scene in a country' (presumably because Shakespeare was writing successful plays).
1595 A shareholder in 'The Lord Chamberlain's Men', an acting company that became extremely popular.
1596 Son Hamnet dies, aged eleven.
Father, John, granted arms (acknowledged as a gentleman).
1597 Buys New Place, the grandest house in Stratford.
1598 Acts in Ben Jonson's *Every Man in His Humour.*
1599 Globe Theatre opens on Bankside. Performances in the open air.
1601 Father, John, dies.
1603 James I grants Shakespeare's company a royal patent: 'The Lord Chamberlain's Men' became 'The King's Men' and played about twelve performances each year at court.
1607 Daughter, Susanna, marries Dr John Hall.
1608 Mother, Mary, dies.
1609 'The King's Men' begin performing indoors at Blackfriars Theatre.
1610 Probably returned from London to live in Stratford.
1616 Daughter, Judith, marries Thomas Quiney.
Dies. Buried in Holy Trinity Church, Stratford-upon-Avon.

## The plays and poems
(no one knows exactly when he wrote each play)

1589–1595 *The Two Gentlemen of Verona, The Taming of the Shrew, First, Second and Third Parts of King Henry VI, Titus Andronicus, King Richard III, The Comedy of Errors, Love's Labour's Lost, A Midsummer Night's Dream, Romeo and Juliet, King Richard II* (and the long poems *Venus and Adonis* and *The Rape of Lucrece*).

1596–1599 *King John, The Merchant of Venice, First and Second Parts of King Henry IV, The Merry Wives of Windsor, Much Ado About Nothing, King Henry V, Julius Caesar* (and probably the *Sonnets*).

1600–1605 *As You Like It, Hamlet, Twelfth Night, Troilus and Cressida, Measure for Measure, Othello, All's Well That Ends Well, Timon of Athens, King Lear.*

1606–1611 *Macbeth, Antony and Cleopatra, Pericles, Coriolanus, The Winter's Tale, Cymbeline, The Tempest.*

1613 *King Henry VIII, The Two Noble Kinsmen* (both probably with John Fletcher).

1623 Shakespeare's plays published as a collection (now called the First Folio).